Doing Church as a Team

A PUBLICATION OF
NEW HOPE RESOURCES

DOING CHURCH AS A TEAM
Published by New Hope Publishers.
A publication of New Hope Resources.
Copyright ©1998 by Wayne Cordeiro.

ISBN 0-9654251-3-4
Unless otherwise indicated, Scripture is from the NEW AMERICAN STANDARD BIBLE ®, Copyright © The Lockman Foundation 1960, 1962, 1963, 1968, 1971, 1972, 1973, 1975, 1977. Used by permission.

Managing Editor: Carole Ka'apu
Editorial Team: Steffany Shima Perez, Dawn O'Brien,
        Randy Furushima, and Glenn White.
Design & Layout: Bernie Kim

First Printing: January 1998
Second Printing: July 1998
Third Printing: May 1999

Published by New Hope Resources
New Hope Christian Fellowship O'ahu.
2826 Kaihikapu St., 2nd Floor
Honolulu, HI 96819-2010

Printed in the United States of America.

Contents

Acknowledgements

I want to say *mahalo* (Hawaiian for "thank you") to the many people who have given me input and inspiration for this book. Whether they've realized it or not, I have been mentored by scores of wonderful people who may never win a prize or get their name in print. These are my silent heroes, people who have jewel-studded crowns awaiting them from the One they serve so willingly.

Thank you to the many that have taught me along the way. To the wonderful New Hope Churches in the Pacific Rim: you are my family. To Clarke Bright, Randy Furushima, Creighton Daniel Arita, and Guy Higashi for making it all come together. Thank you for always reaching for God's best and never saying that it couldn't be done! I asked you to reach high, and you touched the heavens with your heart's response. I have learned so much as we've partnered together. What a ride!

To Bernie Kim for your heart and art, Kaydi Fukunaga for your wonderful volunteers whom you serve so well, and to the famous, ... or is it infamous, interns of New Hope: Darrin, Jeremy, Blaine, Toru, Talo, and Isaku. To Randy and Steffany for their editing team. To Eva and Bertram, Linda DeCosta, Carole Ka'apu, the Iranons, Kapurs, Takakis, and Pangs for your dear friendship.

To Steve and Cindy Kenny, Colleen Nomura, Dane Ison, the Tiltons, and all the wonderful artists, dancers, and musicians of New Hope's Front Lines for your partnership in redeeming the arts. Thank you to Craig Chong and the fantastic "Levites" ministry for following the pillar so willingly through the setting up and taking down of our worship facilities every Sunday! To all the wonderful volunteer teams that are too numerous to mention: Hospitality, 1st Impressions, Care Ministries, Heart 2 Heart, Children's Ministries, Counseling, and dozens more; thank you for who you are. You always remind me of how beautiful the Body of Christ is!

To Mary Hiyama and Doris Aoki for consistently showing me what being a servant is all about. To Pauline Spencer for keeping Jeannie in line and the staff in Hilo for always believing. To Jon Yamazaki for our many travels to Japan as a team, and to Alex Pacheco for the memories at sea as we learned about God's call on our lives.

Thank you to the many others who have shaped my life: the late Dr. Roy Hicks, Jr., Bill Hybels of Willow Creek Community Church, Bruce Bugbee, Bill Gothard, and Rick Warren of Saddleback Community Church. Thank you especially to Dr. Paul Risser who has taught me so many things about developing people skills. You have been a great mentor to me over the years. To Noel Campbell who served tirelessly with me when I began to pioneer churches and to my dear friends Dan and Carol Ann Shima who put their hands to the plow and never looked back. To all the wonderful staff and leaders at New Hope Christian Fellowship in O'ahu who have graciously allowed me to paddle with them. To my dear wife Anna and my children from whom I have learned so much. I have so much yet to learn, but with your love and support, I will never give up! Each of you is a gift to my life, and a gift to the whole Church! ✗

Foreword

Writing a book like this is never an easy task. "Doing Church as a Team" is not some original, innovative new concept. Instead, it is as old as the Bible itself, but hopefully described in contemporary terms. Ecclesiastes tells us that there is nothing new under the sun. We get to learn from each other. Rick Warren, pastor of Saddleback Community Church in California, once quipped, "I offered a man an idea to try, but he declined and told me in no uncertain terms that he was going to either be original or nothing ... so he became both."

It is my deep desire that this book will give leaders the simple steps and necessary handles to put an age-old concept into action. The ideas herein are the accumulation of over twenty-two years in ministry, making hundreds of mistakes, observing dozens of wonderful churches and hundreds of leaders in action. It is the very heart and passion of an amazing church called "New Hope Christian Fellowship" in Oahu, Hawaii. It was our tenth pioneer work since 1984. After two and a half years, the average attendance on Sunday mornings grew to over 5,000. In that number of people, over 3,820 have made first-time commitments to follow Christ, and over 2,600 of those have been baptized.

The church outgrew me in the first month. If it weren't for the outstanding servants whom God brought to serve, I am sure I would be in the mental ward of a state institution by now. (Some still feel I should still enroll, anyway.) Although I had been in ministry at this point for over twenty years, I was more certain than ever that I knew much less than I thought I did! Because of the accelerated growth, "Doing Church as a Team" came almost as a necessity! Yet through all the trials and struggles, a diamond was formed and a gem was fashioned: My heart's desire is to deposit the truths learned here into your account!

This book is written for those, pastors and members of congregations, who have a deep desire to make a difference with their lives. You'll come away motivated and inspired in your walk with the Lord. You will find brand new insights that will encourage you to keep reaching for God's very best. It is written for leaders who, like myself, have found the status quo unacceptable. At various times, I will address pastors, and other times I will address volunteer leaders. But in the final analysis, these truths will apply to every person, every church, and every denomination. This isn't a book on how to become more like a certain church's style, but instead, it is a book on how to become more like the person or church Jesus created you to be. We must learn from each other, and if we do, we'll be miles ahead towards becoming all God created us to be!

How often I have wrestled with the fact that if the Word of God indeed is powerful, then why is the average church in America fewer than one hundred people in attendance every Sunday morning? According to Chuck Colson in a recent speech, he stated that the prison population has tripled in the past five years and crime has increased five hundred and sixty percent! We have over three hundred thousand churches in our country. We can do better. I know we can, and if we join hearts and learn from each other, we can do it! God would have never given us the Great Commission to "go into all the world and preach the Gospel" if He never intended for that to really happen. Peter tells us that He is willing "that none should perish, but for all to come to repentance" (2 Peter 3:9). God would not say that if it weren't possible!

But we cannot do that alone. No pastor can fulfill that calling, regardless of how gifted he may be. Unless every single one of us catches that fire, in the long run there will be no warmth against the chill of the age we're living in.

Jigoro Kano was the founder of the art of Judo and the highest-ranking black belt in this world-renowned sport. Nearing his death, he made one last request of his students when he died. He wanted them to bury him wearing a white belt, the symbol of a beginner, a learner.

My prayer is that we will always be learners. In fact, the word for "disciple" comes from the Greek word, *mathetes*, or learner. Humility and teachability are the crown jewels of all the qualities of a leader that God will use in the next century. May we learn God's design for His people and begin to respect each other's gifting. There are few things more beautiful than seeing God's people serving and working together in a united rhythm. It's like a symphony to His ears. That's how He's created us to function. God designs us in such a way that we are meant to need each other! No one can do it as a solo artist! No one church can reach their community alone. For us to reach everyone, we will need every ministry doing well, every church to be excited, and every congregation doing church as a team!

A dear friend of mine, Tom Paterson, described it in this way. He said, "If I have one good idea, and you have one good idea, how many ideas does each of us have? The answer? One." Then he continued, "Now if I share my idea with you and you share yours with me, how many does each one NOW have? Answer? TWO! You see," he continued with a gleam in his eye, "if we share our idea with each other, we have doubled our knowledge immediately! However have we lost our own idea? No! We still have it. But by sharing, we have increased our knowledge 100%!"

I am learning that I cannot be fulfilled apart from other people. In fact, the bottom line of this whole book is this: you can't do it alone. If you want to be a successful leader, if you plan to have a successful ministry, you must develop not only your gifts, but also the gifts of others around you. If you give your life away, you'll end up discovering what life is all about!

Jesus' Final Prayer

" ... that they may all be one; even as Thou, Father, art in Me, and I in Thee, that they also may be in Us, that the world may believe that Thou didst send Me" (Jn. 17:21).

This is one of Jesus' final prayers for the Church before He was betrayed and crucified. I often notice that as Christians, we are constantly asking God to answer our prayers. There's nothing inherently wrong with that. He is so faithful to answer, but after reading this verse, I thought, "Wouldn't it be nice if once, just for once, we could answer one of HIS prayers!?"

Doing church as a team is one of the ways we can do that. That's what this book is all about. After all, He's answered hundreds and hundreds of our prayers!

Now maybe, just maybe, we can finally answer one of His! ✗

Introduction
Experiencing the Rhythm

In 1984, we moved our family to the Big Island of Hawaii. I had lived in Oregon during my junior high school years after being raised in the Palolo Valley of Oahu. After Bible College and ten years in the youth ministry, God placed an undeniable call on my heart to return and shepherd the people in a beautiful community called Hilo. Nestled between the two mountains of Mauna Kea and Mauna Loa, Hilo is one of the most beautiful cities in the islands. Stretching out eastward is a natural bay that has welcomed some of the first missionaries to Hawaii as well as other sea faring visitors for decades. Lying at the foot of these two imposing mountains (usually topped with snow each winter), Hilo becomes the recipient of constant rain showers giving it the distinct reputation of being the wettest city in the United States. It has an average annual rainfall of over one hundred and twenty inches!

Hilo also has some of the most beautiful people in the world. They are fun loving, relationship-oriented people with much *aloha*, or love for one another. They enjoy sports, fishing, eating, music and laughter.

One of the more popular sports is canoe paddling. There are six paddlers in a canoe with a balancing arm called an *ama*. Although navigating one of these ancient canoes may look basic, the technique required is much more than meets the eye.

A few summers ago, six of us from the church were invited to compete as a crew in an upcoming race. We were game for something new, so we acquired Russell Chin, one of the canoe instructors from a nearby club. We started our first lesson in an adjacent lake of brackish water. Russell sat astride the nose of the canoe facing us as he called out his signals and instructions.

We were in our places, and the first lesson began.

"OK, everyone!" he yelled. "This is how you hold a paddle!" he said, modeling the correct form. As we were figuring out which end we were to grasp and with what hand, he continued.

"We're going to paddle our first stretch of water. It will be an eighth of a mile sprint. When I begin the stopwatch and say 'go,' just paddle as fast and hard as you can. When we cross the finish line, I'll notify you. That's when you can stop paddling. Got it?"

"How hard can this be?" I thought. "Even women paddle canoes. This ought to be a breeze!"

Just then, my self-confident thoughts were shattered by the sharp call of our coach.

"Ho'omakaukau? Imua!"

In English, it means, "Ready? Go forward!"

With our muscles bulging and sinews stretched, we burst out of our dead-in-the-water starting position like a drowning elephant trying to get air. We thrashed our paddles on either side of the canoe. Not knowing when to switch from one side to the other, we figured the best time would simply be when one arm got tired. So, firing at will, I crossed the blade of my oar over and across the canoe, and when I did, I scraped the back of my fellow paddler, Roy Pua-Kaipo, seated directly in front of me. He grunted as my oar etched an unmistakable red mark across his spine. But Roy didn't stop. He just kept beating the water like a trooper. We were on a crusade!

It felt as if hours had transpired. My arms became like lead and my lungs were on fire. Roy's back was starting to bleed, and our canoe was half filled with water. The elephant was beginning to drown when we finally heard Russell yell, "OK, stop!"

"Thank God!" I thought. We abandoned the sinking canoe as our bodies slumped into the brackish water, totally exhausted.

"One minute, forty-two seconds!" Russell yelled. "Pretty sad!"

Like war-torn warriors, we comforted each other, apologizing for the scrapes and wounds from the flailing paddles. We started bailing the water out of our canoe that had begun to resemble more a defeated submarine than that of a sleek racing vessel.

Russell gathered us whimpering novices together, and after a few basics about safety, he taught us how to paddle as a team. Each fledgling paddler was to mirror the one in front of him and everyone in time with the lead stroker. He taught us how to switch our paddles without injuring each other. We practiced together again and again until our stroking became as rhythmic as a metronome. We were beginning to look good! After a few practice runs, our coach took us back to our original starting position.

"All right!" said Russell. "Let's try that same eighth mile stretch again. Only this time, I want you to stroke as if you were taking a leisurely stroll through the park. No sprinting. Just mirror the one in front of you and switch with a smooth cadence of rhythm, just as you were taught! Stroke as a team and don't try to break any sound barriers this time, OK? Ready?"

With a confidence, we took our mark. He barked out the starting signal. *"Ho'omakaukau? Imua!"*

Our oars silently entered the water in perfect timing. Mike Diaz, the lead stroker called out his command. "Hut!" In perfect chorus, we answered, "Ho!" and we were off.

Our canoe cut through the water like a knife blade goes through jelly. We switched sides without skipping a beat. We mirrored the one in front of us. We were being transformed from a drowning circus animal into a precision machine! Then, just as we were feeling the exhilaration of smooth progress, Russell yelled, "OK! Stop paddling."

The ahead-of-expected arrival caught all of us by surprise.

"Anybody tired?"

We all shook our heads, "No!"

He held up his stopwatch so we could see it, then exclaimed, "You beat your last time by twenty-four seconds!"

I couldn't believe it! Nobody was injured! No one went overboard out of sheer exhaustion! No canoe deluged with water! No fire in my lungs! It was a sheer delight! We congratulated each other, gave a few victory shouts, exchanged leis and took pictures! This was amazing!

And we did it together! We paddled as a team!

Doing Church as a Team

Just like paddling a canoe, God designed us to stroke together. He has designed each church with a special purpose, and His plan is to saturate the carrying out of that ministry with joy!

In order for this to happen, God gives each of us a unique gift. The combination of these gifts working in synch should bring such a radiance that the whole world would stand up and take notice!

Each of us has been given a "paddle" by God. A gift. A calling. And like the paddlers of a canoe, each of us has a place or a role to fill. On each paddle is our unique thumbprint, our own individual circuitry, designed by God Himself. He then places each of us in a community, and more specifically in a local church with a divine purpose. He fits us alongside others who have a similar assignment and calls us a family, a team, the Church. No one person is meant to carry this assignment alone. It wasn't designed that way. We were created to do church as a team!

A full symphony under the direction of a master conductor will always sound infinitely better than a one-man band. As we discover and develop our individual gifts and learn to stroke in rhythm as a team, we'll be absolutely astonished at how much further we'll get ... and with fewer injuries! ✕

God Has a Plan!

God Has a Plan!

You could have been born in another place and another time!

God doesn't do things at random. Like God did with Jeremiah, He planned your birth before you were even conceived! He chose you, created you, and then delicately placed you on His sovereign time continuum.

God never makes mistakes. I have searched the Bible thoroughly, and I have yet to find even one instance where God ever said, "Oops!" Sorry, you won't find that word in any concordance.

If God wanted to, isn't it true that He could have created you to have been born in the 10th century? You could have been born in any of the years before Christ. But for some reason, He wanted you born and living in this age, in this century, in this day called "today." He has a purpose and a plan for you!

If He wanted to, He could have had you placed in another nation. You could be living in Europe or Africa, speaking not English, but Swahili, or Hungarian! But for some reason, He has you and me in the nation of the United States of America.

Let's take this a step further. Of all the states in this nation that you could be living in, He has chosen you to live in the one you are in right now! For me and a group of people in New Hope, it's Hawaii! (Thank God!)

But have you ever seen Hawaii on a globe? You can hardly find the place! For many years, I thought Hawaii was located just off the tip of Alaska because on every map I saw while growing up, Hawaii was in a small box located just off the Alaskan coastline! But still, of all the landmasses on this globe, He chose a tiny grouping of islands for us to reside on ... the state of Hawaii!

Not only did God pre-select the state you are living in right now, but He even chose the city! He didn't place you in just any city. He placed you in the very city where you now reside! And furthermore, just think of this. Of all the churches He could have put you in, He's placed you in one certain, specific church!

I think that's a miracle!

"From one man he made every nation of men, that they should inhabit the whole earth; and he determined the times set for them and the exact places where they should live" (Acts 17:26 NIV).

God doesn't make any mistakes. He has a plan! We find it written: "For we are His workmanship, created in Christ Jesus for good works, which God prepared beforehand, that we should walk in them" (Eph. 2:10).

God prepared our paths "beforehand" that we should walk in them! He has a plan for each and every one of us, and it is our responsibility to find out what that is and then, walk in it!

> "You did not choose Me, but I chose you, and appointed you, that you should go and bear fruit, and that your fruit should remain..." (Jn. 15:16).

God chose you for a very specific purpose. If God didn't have a special purpose for you and if He didn't want you to succeed, then He wouldn't have had you born! He wouldn't have created you! Sometimes we read in the newspapers of those who get so depressed that they end up taking their own lives. They lose their reason to live, and suicide becomes the quickest escape route from the pain.

Did God make some cosmic mistake? Did each of these people with tragic endings really have a life empty of purpose?

God never makes mistakes. Never! And by the way, you didn't choose Him. God chose you and appointed you that you should be fruitful with your life. So don't settle for anything less. You have one life to live on this earth, and it comes with a special commission on it. Invest it wisely. Don't squander it or misuse it!

Only One Life to Give

This globe that we're riding on called Mother Earth is not as still as it may appear. It's traveling at over 60,000 miles per hour! That's right! The rotation of this earth is spinning faster than the wring-cycle of your washing machine. "Time sure flies" is more than a trite phrase. That's why the Psalmist describes our life to be as transient as our "breath." Job says it is but a "sigh." James likens it to a "vapor that appears today and is gone tomorrow." Our life is indeed "flashing before our eyes!" A few more spins, and our life will be over. We'll be in eternity!

What is eternity like? The Bible tells us that Jesus paid dearly for something called eternal life that He made available to each of us. What is it like?

Comparing our life on this earth with the eternity that Jesus purchased for us, I would describe it in this way.

Imagine that you took a cable and shot it in one direction. This cable went straight toward the horizon until the end was out of sight. Then you took the other end and shot it in the opposite direction. Let's say the cable stretches through the room you're in and is directly in front of you. It passes through both of the walls on each side of the room and stretches into infinity. Now that's what eternity is like! Eternity, like the cable, is forever extending in both directions with no end in sight.

What's our life like on this earth? To contrast the brevity of our earthly dwelling with that of eternity, I would take out my ballpoint pen and draw a vertical scratch on the extended cable. Then I would tell you that the width of that vertical scratch (about 1/32nd of an inch) is about how long our life is on this earth in comparison with eternity. That's right. Not very long!

But do you know what most people do? They not only live on that scratch, but they love that scratch. They kiss the scratch. They save for that scratch. They hoard for that scratch. They live scratch lives, have scratch businesses, and have scratch families with scratch hopes and scratch dreams.

But God so loved that scratch that He sent His only begotten Son to die for those who live there. Yet many still don't know about this "gift" called eternal life! They're still hanging on to the scratch. They try to elongate it, stretch it, and extend their scratch lives as much as possible. But even in the midst of their attempts, they know deep inside that there's got to be something more!

The Bible says "God put eternity in the heart of every man" (Eccl. 3:11 paraphrased). This is why each person longs for more than what the world can offer. There is the classic quote that says there is a "God shaped void" in the heart of every man. Although many try to fill it with material possessions, drugs, or alcohol, only God Himself can fill that aching chasm.

The fact that you are reading this is a good sign that you have heard His invitation and have chosen to follow Him. You are saved! What an amazing grace He's extended to you and me! But that's not all there is! Let me tell you ... the rest of the story.

God's Reason for Saving Us

What was God's reason for saving you? Was it just to get you to heaven? Was that the only reason He sent His Son? Absolutely not!

If getting you to heaven were God's only reason for saving you, then the moment you would have received Christ as your Lord and Savior, God would have killed you! That's right. Now that you are saved, His job would be complete. He might as well get you on to heaven! There'd be no use for you hanging around here any longer!

But that wasn't the only reason He saved you. Instead of taking you immediately home, He placed a message in your heart ... a message of "Good News" about the eternal life that God has prepared for anyone "who would call upon the Name of the Lord!" Then He put you back on that scratch for a few more spins. But now there's a purpose to your life. There's a plan He has for you! Soon, your life and mine will be over, but until He takes us home, we have a message to deliver!

Someone once said, "We will have all of eternity to boast about the victories won on the earth, but we have only a few hours left in which to win them!" I agree!

When we get to heaven, we will see many wonderful things, but let me tell you of one thing we will never see again. We will never see another non-Christian. We will never have another opportunity for the rest of eternity to share the Good News with someone who desperately needs the grace of God. The joy of heaven is when people come to a saving faith in Christ! These are the victories! Now, what in the world would we talk about for all of eternity if when we arrive, we've not been "about our Father's business?" We must accomplish what God sent us onto this scratch to accomplish!

His Plan—Our Responsibility

A story is told of a Christian nurse who attended a very sick man confined to the Intensive Care Unit of a hospital. Although only in his early sixties, death seemed to loom closer with each passing day. The nurse would share the Lord with him and pray fervently for his salvation and healing. As the days slipped by, so did his chances for recovery. One evening, his breathing became so labored that the doctors feared he wouldn't make it through the night. His nurse spent extra hours that evening by his bedside praying for his healing.

The following morning, the nurse arrived back at work expecting to find an empty bed. But to her surprise, instead of an empty bed, she found her patient sitting up in remarkable health, eating breakfast! She was overjoyed!

"Praise the Lord!" she exclaimed! "You're healed!"

"Yup!" he cheerfully replied. "I feel great. You and your prayers ... you healed me!"

"Oh no! I didn't heal you," she quickly replied. "God did. And now, it is your responsibility to find out why!"

Personal Application

God didn't save us so we could have access to someone who would answer all our prayers. God is not a genie in a lamp that is ever available to answer our every whim. We are His servants. We belong to Him, and we exist for His purposes ... not the other way around. He has saved us and given each of us a second chance. Now, we must find out why. Isn't it time we pause long enough to recalibrate our heading?

Jesus tells in Mark 8:36: "For what does it profit a man if he gains the whole world, and forfeit his soul?" The application for someone who does not know Christ is obvious, but what is not so obvious is its application for us as Christians! For the Christian it could be applied in this way: "What would it profit a Christian if he gets all his prayers answered (a fine house, abundant income, and blessings galore) but ultimately misses the very reason for which he was created?" Wouldn't that be a waste!

Take a few moments to ask yourself why you think God created you and why He placed you where you are. He makes no mistakes. You are on "special assignment" during your stay here on earth. As you read this book, let Him reveal to you what that is! He will. You watch, you wait, you'll see! ✗

CHAPTER ONE STUDY GUIDE

"God Has a Plan!"

1. Read John 15:16. God chose each of us for a reason. If God were to tell you six things that He would want your life to stand for, what would they be?

   a.

   b.

   c.

   d.

   e.

   f.

2. Why do you think God gave you certain gifts and placed you in a specific church?

3. What is one thing you would want to accomplish before God takes you home? Write it below as a prayer.

CHAPTER TWO

Don't Forget
Who You Are

Chapter Two
Don't Forget Who You Are

"For our citizenship is in heaven..." (Phil. 3:20).

There's an old story of a rabbi in a Russian city at the turn of the century. Disappointed by a lack of direction and purpose, he wandered out into the chilly evening. With his hands thrust deep into his pockets, he aimlessly walked through the empty streets questioning his faith in God, the Scriptures, and his calling to ministry. The only thing colder than the Russian winter air was the chill within his own soul. He was so enshrouded by his own despair that he mistakenly wandered into a Russian military compound, off limits to any civilians.

Just then the silence of the evening chill was shattered by the bark of a Russian soldier.

"Who are you? And what are you doing here?!" he yelled.

"Excuse me?" replied the rabbi.

"I said, 'Who are you and what are you doing here?!'"

After a brief moment, the rabbi in a gracious tone so as not to evoke any anger from the soldier said, "How much do you get paid every day?"

"What does that have to do with you?" he retorted.

The rabbi replied, with a tone resembling that of someone who just made a new discovery, "I will pay you the equal sum if you will ask me those same two questions every day: 'Who are you?' and 'What are you doing here?'"

Let me be that Russian soldier for you over these next few pages as I ask you those same two questions:

"Who are you, and what are you doing here?"

Just Like the Israelites

One of Israel's most recurring problems was forgetfulness. Forgetting who they were and thus forgetting the God they served became a common malady. How often we find in the Old Testament the Lord needing to remind them of who they were. He reminds them in Deuteronomy, "Beware lest you forget the Lord your God..." (Deut. 8:11).

A few verses later in that same book, God sternly warned the Israelites that if they should forget, the results may be disastrous. "And it shall come about if you ever forget the Lord your God, ... I testify against you today that you shall surely perish. Like the nations that the Lord makes to perish before you..." (Deut. 8:19-20).

Often, we find the Israelites building stone altars in the wilderness signifying a spot where God had done something spectacular, either a miracle of provision or one of victory. Ever wonder why? It was a way God tried to remind them of who they were and what they were supposed to be doing here! Directly after a miracle would have occurred, God would order them to build an altar of stones so that "in years to come when your sons shall ask you 'Who are we and what are we doing here?' you shall tell them!"

Forgetting Who We Are Should Scare Us!

A few summers ago, my son Aaron and three of his friends found a fifty-five-gallon barrel and a sloping hill. The combination of those two discoveries by a group of teenage boys can spell mischief. And so it did. They thought it would be great fun getting inside the barrel and rolling one another down the hill. The first to volunteer his life and future was none other than Aaron. (I think he got that bravery from his mother.)

The barrel took off from a slow, labored roll and soon accelerated into an out-of-control, warp-speed, one-man suicide mission. The barrel surged down the hill, flipping end over end until it came to a crashing halt. Somewhere along the wild ride, Aaron hit his head on the side of the flying barrel and it knocked him out cold. When he finally regained consciousness, he couldn't remember a thing! He sustained a concussion, and his memory was gone!

I was at a meeting when I received a "911" call from one of his friends (and partners in crime) that Aaron was at home. He reported that Aaron had hit his head and had no recollection of anything that took place. I rushed home immediately only to find a very frightened sixteen-year-old boy who had temporary amnesia due to the concussion. Although he's a virile, strapping young man, I had never seen him so afraid.

"Dad, I can't remember anything!" he said through the tears. "I'm so scared!"

I tried reassuring him that his erased memory was only a temporary loss, and in a day or so, it would return. The memory of the event itself may not, but everything else should be fine. But even with my best efforts to assure him, he remained scared and unsure.

Well, we drove him to the emergency room and I had the dubious honor of trying to explain to the attending physicians how this concussion had come about. The doctors wheeled him into another room for a CAT scan. About an hour later, the Emergency Room physician returned. He informed us that Aaron's memory would return in a day or two and that the scan of his brain came back "normal" ... (which frankly, surprised me!) I was shocked that they found anything normal in there at all! In fact, I suggested that it might be beneficial for each of his friends to take one of those scans. I thought that the accumulative total of all four brains should have at least equaled one in the whole bunch!

We took Aaron home, and just like Dad had diagnosed, the following day his memory was back to normal, all except the immediate event itself. But I will always remember how scared he was when he lost his memory of who he was!

Israel had this recurring problem, but no alarms went off and no buzzers sounded. No one, except for an occasional lone-voiced prophet, even noticed that anything might be wrong! In the same way, God has given us an identity and a purpose for living. Never forget why God saved you!

> *When we forget who we are,*
> *it should scare us!*

I'm glad Aaron recuperated from his injury, and he came through with a little more wisdom about empty 55-gallon barrels, sloping hills, and willing friends who nominate one another.

And how was I so certain about the diagnosis of his injury? How could his father speak with such authority that he'd make it through? How could I have such confidence in the fact that his memory would return within twenty-four hours?

I'll let you figure that one out for yourself...

Every Member is a Minister

"And He Himself gave some to be ... pastors and teachers, for the equipping of the saints for the work of the ministry" (Eph. 4:11-12 NKJV).

In doing church as a team, this next principle is one of the most important. In Ephesians, Paul calls us "saints". I always thought saints were those brave and wonderful Christians of years past who lived miraculously and then died for their faith. Instead, the Bible talks about us being saints, the people who are alive and doing the work of the ministry! In the New Testament, God identifies Christians as the saints. He calls each of us a "minister." In fact, He even goes so far as to call us a "royal priesthood" in 1 Peter 2:9!

But somewhere along the line, we've forgotten who God created us to be. Instead of us fulfilling our own calling, tradition has taught us to hire others to do that for us. We would interview a potential "reverend," and if he could preach and do the business of the church, we would hire him. Then after a few years, if he did an adequate job of preaching, visiting the sick, performing weddings and funerals, we would vote to "renew his call." He was the one that was supposed to do the ministry, and so we just stepped out of his way.

Over the decades, we've instituted the professional "clergy" and simultaneously, we developed a new breed of churchgoers called "consumer Christians."

A consumer Christian can easily be spotted traveling from church to church, shopping for bargains and filling their empty baskets of expectations with programs and personalities. Then after a reasonable period of searching, they settle on the one that most adequately fits the bill. They then begin to "consume," and if at any time their rate of consumption is not equaled by the church's rate of feeding, they pack up and begin the search routine all over again.

Maybe it's time we return to the way God designed the Church to function in the first place. Maybe it's time we realize that the ministry of the Church is not the responsibility of a few professionals. Instead, it is the divine responsibility of every single one of us!

Every member is a minister. That's what God says. In fact, He calls us full-time ministers! Full-time? Yes! Not just on Sundays. Not just at Bible studies, but full-time!

Do we love God just "part-time"? Do we serve Him just "part-time"? We are all full-time citizens of heaven with a commission and an assignment to accomplish during our stay here on earth.

Before you are a businessman, you are a minister. Before you are a homemaker, you are a minister. Before you are a student, a grandparent, a CEO, you are firstly a minister.

Some may ask, "But I don't work for the church! I work for the State (or the police department, a construction company, the Department of Education, or a manufacturing firm). My company pays me, not my church! How can you say that I am a full-time minister?"

The Source of All Our Provision

Sometimes we mistake the *channel* of our provision for the *source* of our provision. The Bible tells us that "God is our Provider," not a company or business. In fact, if you would trace your paycheck back to its true source, you will find that it may take you to your place of employment, but it doesn't stop there! Like tracing a stereo wire, you'll find that if you keep following it, all our paychecks can be traced back to the very Throne of God!

He is our Provider. He may choose to use various places of employment through which He provides, but it is He Who provides! Even though you might be self-employed, He reminds us in Deuteronomy 8:18, "But you shall remember (there's our word again!) the Lord your God, for it is He who is giving you the power to make wealth.."

What's the Best Way to Reach People?

"...and he determined the times set for them and the exact places where they should live. God did this so that men would seek him and perhaps reach out for him and find him" (Acts 17: 26b-27 NIV).

Have you ever asked yourself, "How does God plan to reach all the people living in my community? Look again at Acts 17:26b-27. God really has a plan. Yet so often we might look at the overwhelming task of reaching our community and feel helpless. We simply shrug our shoulders and wonder to ourselves, "There's so many people scattered everywhere! And there's only one 'minister' in our little church to try and reach them all!"

Doing church as a team has a whole new way of looking at this dilemma.

Do you believe that God loves policemen? I do. Do you believe that He loves teachers? Me, too. What about construction workers? Absolutely! In fact, the Bible says, "The Lord is ... not wishing for any to perish, but for ALL to come to repentance" (2 Peter 3:9 emphasis added). And if He truly does love them and wants to reach them with the Good News, then what would be the very best way to do that? Through a pastor?

Possibly, but that may not be the most ideal. People at your office or school may be quite intimidated if the pastor walked into the lunchroom and began preaching. What's the best way to reach teachers?

The best way would obviously be through another teacher!

So what does God do?

He takes "full-time ministers" and disguises them as teachers! Yup! He takes saints like you and me, and He gives them gifts and passions to be the best teachers they can be. Then He sends them into the school system in order to reach other educators with God's love!

How does God reach police officers? He takes "full-time ministers" and disguises them as police officers. He gives them the gifts and passions, the credentials necessary, and spins them off into various police departments all over the nation. How does He reach construction workers? He takes "full-time ministers" and disguises them as construction workers. He gives them the gifts and passions, makes them strong and hairy (... excluding women construction workers, of course!), and He distributes them into different construction companies throughout every city. Why? Because this is God's plan in reaching construction workers!

God's full-time ministers are everywhere! We are all Ambassadors. We are all ministers. Each one of us is to represent Him in the world, not just pastors or evangelists.

I have the privilege of pastoring a young, vibrant church in Hawaii, but my call to this church is no greater a call than anyone else's! We are all called! We are all ministers! The pastor's role may differ from other roles, but the callings are the same, to be ministers!

So, in every city, every town, and every country, there will be full-time ministers, differently gifted and differently slotted into every business and vocation! And like salt from a salt shaker, God takes us and scatters us everywhere to suit His flavor. He "salts" the earth with His ministers, He gives them gifts with which to influence their friends, families, co-workers, and as the old hymn-writer composed, to reach: "Every kindred, every tribe on this terrestrial ball!"

"You are the salt of the earth; but if the salt has become tasteless, how will it be made salty again? It is good for nothing anymore, except to be thrown out and trampled underfoot..." (Mt. 5:13).

Don't lose your savor and don't forget who you are! ✗

CHAPTER TWO STUDY GUIDE

"Don't Forget Who You Are"

1. "Who are you and what are you doing here?" If you were to answer this question, what would your answer be?

2. The Israelites had a recurring problem of forgetting who God called them to be. Even with all the miracles and with all their feast days, still they would wander off. What do you think caused this?

3. Do you agree that "every member is a minister?" Read Ephesians 4:11-12. What will it take for the people in our churches to catch this and rise to the challenge?

4. Whether you are a schoolteacher or a college student, whether among your family or friends, God can use you where you are! Each of us is a full-time minister. What are some ways God is calling you to minister within your unique sphere of influence?

5. Write down three names: one of a coworker or fellow student, an unsaved family member, and an unsaved friend. Take a few minutes to pray for their salvation. Then ask God for an opportunity to share the gospel with them.

The Gifts:
Commissioned
Beyond Ourselves

Chapter Three

The Gifts: Commissioned Beyond Ourselves

No Christian is without one. It may be dormant, underdeveloped, or as yet undiscovered, but each one has at least one!

———•———

God does something very special for everyone entering into His family. He gives each member a divine endowment known as a spiritual gift. This gift is a God-given capacity to fulfill what He has asked us to accomplish. This gift helps us to locate our niche, our place, and our role. Coming to grips with this fact may be one of the most wonderful discoveries of your life!

Assigning someone with a task and equipping someone for the same are completely different issues. God knew that if we were to accomplish His will, we would not be able to do it on our own strength. We would need something greater than ourselves! Even if we, on our own strength, happened to gain even a miniscule amount of success, pride would swell us up like a toad.

Gideon was like that, wasn't he? God asked him to fight against a marauding band of raiders called the Midianites. Prior to the battle however, God deemed it necessary to prune Gideon's army from 32,000 warriors to a measly 300! When Gideon asked God for the reason behind this seemingly suicidal decision, God answered with these words: "The people who are with you are too many for Me to give Midian into their hands, lest Israel become boastful, saying, 'My own power has delivered me'" (Judges 7:2).

God loves to take ordinary people like you and me through whom He does extraordinary things! He doesn't need superheroes. He is looking for everyday, willing vessels that He can equip and gift. And moreover, God is so wonderful! He not only gives us divine endowments, but He even supplies the willingness to use them! Paul reminds us of that in Philippians 2:13, "For it is God who is at work in you, both to **will** and to work for His good pleasure" (emphasis added). When we function in the way God gifted us to function, we can accomplish great things. And at the same time, we find great joy in doing His will and His work!

God's Promise to Us

Now concerning spiritual gifts, brethren, I do not want you to be unaware" (1 Cor. 12:1).

God has given each believer specific spiritual gifts to be discovered, developed, and deployed! No Christian is without one. It may be dormant, underdeveloped, or as yet undiscovered, but we all have at least one! And God doesn't want us to be unaware of them. Why? Because knowing and functioning in your gift is at the very heart of the Church.

In doing church as a team, it's not one person doing a hundred things. That's how pastors burn out. It's a hundred people doing one thing each! And that is not only possible, that is how God created us!

The question is not whether we have gifts. We all have at least one! The real issue is whether we know what they are and whether we are developing them for the Master's use. Take a look at the following two scripture verses:

"And since we have gifts that differ according to the grace given to us, let each exercise them accordingly" (Rom. 12:6 emphasis added).

"As each one has received a special gift, employ it in serving one another, as good stewards of the manifold grace of God" (1 Pet. 4:10 emphasis added).

God has equipped us to serve through the use of our gifts, and if we are unaware of them, our ability to serve Him will be immensely impeded. God knew beforehand that His plan could never be accomplished by an act of human will. It could only be accomplished through the strength He supplied in the form of spiritual gifts.

Let's take a closer look at how God equips His people. The Bible mentions three basic categories of gifts.

The Office Gifts

But to each one of us grace was given according to the measure of Christ's gift. Therefore it says:

'When He ascended on high, He led captive a host of captives, and **He gave gifts to men**.' And He gave some as apostles, and some as prophets, and some as evangelists and some as pastors and teachers, for the **equipping** of the saints for the work of service, to the building up of the body of Christ..." (Eph. 4:7-8,11-12 emphasis added).

God put specific offices in the Church for the sake of oversight and leadership. Leadership is not exclusively reserved for these positions, but it is often carried out through them. However, what is of more interest to us in doing church as a team, is the use of the word *equipping*. The role of these offices is not necessarily to capture a corner on the market of ministry. They are offices whose designated role is to equip God's people to do the work of the ministry.

The word equip in the Greek is a very picturesque one. It is the word *katartismon*, meaning, "to mend." It is found in Mark 1:19 as James and John were in the boat with their father Zebedee, "mending their nets." The same word is used in Ephesians 4 that is translated equipping. James and John were mending their nets, or equipping them in order to catch more fish. The nets, simply by reason of use, may have gotten snagged on the rocky bottom of Galilee, and now they were being mended before the next fishing trip. The nets were being equipped for the purpose they were created for ... to catch fish!

Pastors have the same role. They mend saints and they equip them. There will be many instances when hearing the Word of God on Sunday, or at other gatherings, will "mend" you. Its truths will impact you in such a way that it will bring wholeness and healing to an area of your life and relationships. Also through God's Word, you will be increasingly equipped for the purposes God has for you. The messages will challenge you, remind you of who you are, and call you forward to use the gifts He's given you!

A fisherman does not mend his nets just to collect more mended nets! Neither is his goal is to compete with other fishermen in seeing who can collect the biggest pile of nets. That would be ludicrous! He doesn't mend nets to display them on his wall as trophies. What is a fisherman's goal for mending torn nets?

That's right! He mends them in order to throw them back in the lake to catch more fish. That's the whole reason for mending nets!

And the same is true with each of us. God mends us through the office gifts so that we will be equipped to do the work of the ministry. We are equipped so we can "go into all the world." We are strengthened in order to discover and develop our gifting, then "employ it in serving one another as good stewards." (1 Peter 4:10). The Bible says that as we do, the body of Christ will be built up. That's how churches grow! When we are being consistently mended and equipped by the Word of God so that the work of the ministry is being done, churches become vibrant and healthy. That's one of the keys to biblical church growth.

But there are yet more gifts to discover.

Serving Gifts

"And since we have gifts that differ according to the grace given to us, let each exercise them accordingly: if prophecy, according to the proportion of his faith; if service, in his serving; or he who teaches, in his teaching; or he who exhorts, in his exhortation; he who gives, with liberality; he who leads, with diligence; he who shows mercy, with cheerfulness" (Romans 12:6-8).

These gifts are distributed among Christians equipping us to excel in our serving. These we must discover, develop, and deploy. For example, God says that if your gift is teaching, then you must teach! If your gift is serving, then by all means, find a place and start serving! If your gift is leading, then for the sake of the Kingdom of God, lead! In other words, to possess a gift and not use it is unthinkable to God.

Each of us must take the responsibility for the discovery, development and usage of our gifts. The ministry and assignment of any church belongs to the people. As each of us discovers and begins using our gifts, God is honored, the body of Christ is built up, and we begin to sense a fulfillment greater than ever before.

Here we find one of the Apostle Paul's life-long goals:

"Not that I have already obtained it, or have already become perfect, but I press on in order that I may lay hold of that for which also I was laid hold of by Christ Jesus" (Phil. 3:12).

Here, Paul is saying his goal in life was to discover the reason for his God-ordained birth! The reason, as Paul pursues his gifting, was to pioneer churches. His gift of apostleship was expressed in his passion to pioneer churches and to take the Gospel to the Gentiles. God had chosen him for a specific purpose, gifted him for a specific reason, and Paul wasn't about to "go home" until he had fulfilled what God had laid hold of him for!

Serving in Your Passion

Allow me for a moment to take a slight detour and talk about a divine exclamation point that comes with using what God gives us. Along with special gifts, God gives to each of us certain passions, or arenas of service that motivate us more than others. We've all seen musicians who have a passion for the piano above other musical instruments. Therefore they play the piano with a passion! We've all known gifted athletes who are outstanding in one certain sport. They may possess the ability to excel in many different venues, but one certain sport catches their fancy more than the others do. Then into this one sport they pour all their time and energies. They excel in it and play it with passion!

Your passion is the area or arena where you feel most motivated to use your gift. Knowing your spiritual gift will answer the "What?" question, and your passion will answer the "Where?"question.

- Where shall I use my gifts?

- Where do I feel most motivated to serve?

- Where do I sense a calling toward or an attraction for?

> *When you are operating in your gift and passion, you will experience maximum effectiveness and minimum weariness.*

For some, their gift may be serving, and their *passion* is to help elderly people. For another, their gift may be teaching, and their *passion* is discipleship. Therefore, they may be drawn to a small group ministry. Another person's gift may be music, and their passion is working with children. Therefore, they may lead music in the children's ministry.

> *When you are <u>not</u> operating in your gift and passion, you will experience maximum weariness and minimum effectiveness.*

When you link your gifts with your passion, you begin to play a powerful role in the body of Christ. You will find such joy and motivation when this is taking place. In fact, when you are operating in your gift and passion, you will experience maximum effectiveness and minimum weariness. On the other hand, when you are operating outside of your gift or passion, you will experience maximum weariness and minimum effectiveness. I'm sure every person reading this book has felt that kind of strain at one time or another!

The Charismatic Gifts

"Now there are a variety of gifts, but the same Spirit. For to one is given the word of wisdom through the Spirit, and to another the word of knowledge according to the same Spirit; to another faith by the same Spirit, and to another gifts of healing by the one Spirit, and to another the effecting of miracles, and to another prophecy, and to another the distinguishing of spirits, to another various kinds of tongues, and to another the interpretation of tongues. But one and the same Spirit works all these things, distributing to each one individually just as He wills" (1 Cor. 12:4, 8-11).

This third area of gifts may have been the most controversial of all in past years. The interpretation of this section has divided churches, segregated congregations, and generally caused more havoc than whether or not a Christian should "drink, dance, smoke, chew ... or hang around the girls who do."

God has authored every gift by His Spirit and placed them in the Church for the "common good." Each church is designed to have a balance with all the gifts represented and all the gifts functioning. Every gift, whether big or small, seen or unseen, on the platform or in the background, is crucial to the church in order to gain optimum effectiveness. But what did we do?

Somewhere along the way, we gathered all the gifts that looked like "us" and segregated the others. All those with certain gifts, such as "tongues, interpretation of tongues, miracles and prophecy..." (1 Cor. 12:8-11) were grouped together under the label of "Charismatic" or "Pentecostal." They enjoyed each other's company and finally began creating denominations based on their common similarity of gifts.

The "other" group of gifts (Romans 12:6-8) gathered together those who looked like themselves and became known as the "Conservative" corner of the family. For years, they would draw their lines, take their firing pins off safety, and never the twain would meet. The gifts became badges of honor, measurements of spirituality, and terms of endearment.

Often, we will use a measuring rod of evaluation based on how many in a certain congregation agrees with or looks like us! If we enter a new church and they sing, talk, preach, and act like us, that church passes the test, and we will consent to have "fellowship with them." On the other hand, if they don't look like "us" or if they don't meet our expectations of what we had in our minds, then we conclude that this congregation is spiritually lacking, and they are deemed unworthy of our involvement.

But God never said, "Find a church where everyone in it looks like you!" He said, "Find a church where everyone in it looks like Me!"

Much of the segregated thinking that has separated churches from one another in the past is beginning to disappear. Thank God! His original design was for all the gifts to function together, in harmony and with mutual respect. Every gift is necessary for what He desires to accomplish. No one of us alone will possess all the gifts, but together we do! That's called the Church! There's nothing like the church when it is vibrant, healthy, and working like God designed it.

In New Hope, we welcome the totality of the gifts of the Holy Spirit as they were designed to function. We have many with the gift of serving, others with the gift of tongues, others with the gift of leadership, teaching, mercy, giving, word of wisdom, etc. We need each other!

When we need facilities set up or when we need to get a room ready for an activity, those with the gift of serving are always so willing and ready. When a person needs prayer, we all pray, but there's nothing like someone with a gift of intercession who will pray with a passion until the request is answered, and it usually is! When the answer comes, all of us rejoice together.

When we need someone to oversee the hospital ministry, those with a mercy gift will usually be the first to step forward. When decisions are at an impasse, those with the gift of leadership are called upon and they respond with great joy! The impasse is broken and the church moves forward again.

When we need things organized, those who have the gift of organization get excited! They gladly step forward and they do phenomenal things from that which was once chaos! If it weren't for each one willing and using their gifts for the "common good," we'd all be in deep trouble! The more people serve one another through the willing use of their gifts, the more the respect factor for one another goes through the roof. We so need each other!

Neta's Gift

Some months ago, I was to gather a few pastors for a morning meeting. I asked my secretary, Carol Ann, if she could put some water on the tables and enough cups for the dozen pastors who were invited. Now Carol Ann is outstanding at slotting people according to their gifts. Instead of doing something just to barely get by, she called Neta.

Now Neta's gift is hospitality, so when Carol Ann asked if she wouldn't mind coming in and preparing the room, Neta was overjoyed! She picked fresh flowers, lined the tables with beautiful tablecloths, and she had water pitchers filled with fresh, ice cold water ready on the tables. She even had a scarf on each water jug as if they were about to be judged on contemporary pitcher-decor! Selected nuts in little bowls were neatly spaced on the tables with candies and napkins adorning each place setting. The whole room took on a new appearance with the fresh smell of coffee, bagels, and pastries. She had spent all day on preparing the room and making sure that the ambiance was just right, and she loved it!

When I walked into the room on the morning of the meeting, I thought it was a camera shoot for *Better Homes and Gardens*! It was absolutely stunning! The pastors who attended felt so special that "I" would take the time to organize such a beautiful setting just for them. Well, I knew that all the credit went to Neta. Frankly, if it were left to me, there would have been a few paper cups on each table so they could get their own water from the fountain downstairs. That would have sufficed for me, but not for Neta. After the meeting, Neta came up to me and asked, "Do you think you might be having any more of these soon? I just love doing these things!"

You see, Neta's gift is hospitality.

The Danger of Comparing Gifts

One of the common pitfalls that often hinders us from finding our place in the Body of Christ is comparison. We start focusing on what we don't possess rather than investing what we do. We try to look like, sound like, or think like those we admire. But in the end, it only leads to us becoming a frustrated, mediocre version of what we saw. The worst part of it all is that our own creative energies start to dry up.

My wife Anna is from Springfield, Oregon. Some years ago, the *Springfield Public Schools Newsletter* published an article that Chuck Swindoll alluded to in his wonderful book, *A Season of Reflection*. We are once again reminded of how each of us is so uniquely designed by the Master Architect.

Once upon a time, the animals decided they should do something meaningful to meet the problems of the new world. So they organized a school.

They adopted an activity curriculum of running, climbing, swimming and flying. To make it easier to administer, all the animals took all the subjects.

The duck was excellent in swimming. In fact, he was better than his instructor was! However, he made only passing grades in flying, and was very poor in running. Since he was so slow in running, he had to drop swimming and stay after school to practice running. This caused his webbed feet to be badly worn so he became only average in swimming. But "average" was quite acceptable, therefore nobody worried about it - except the duck.

The rabbit started at the top of his class in running, but developed a nervous twitch in his leg muscles because he had so much make-up work to do in swimming.

The squirrel was excellent in climbing, but he encountered constant frustration in flying class because his teacher made him start from the ground up instead of from the treetop down. He developed "charley horses" from overexertion, so he only got a "C" in climbing and a "D" in running.

The eagle was a problem child and was severely disciplined for being a non-conformist. In climbing classes, he beat all the others to the top, but insisted on using his own way of getting there!

The moral of this story is quite obvious. Each of us has been given his or her own gifts, capabilities, and passions that we will be inclined to excel in! If we concentrate only on pointing out each other's weaknesses, we may seem "spiritual" or "vigilant", but not fruitful or helpful.

You see, everybody is a 10 ... somewhere!

By comparing ourselves with one another, we will blind ourselves to the qualities God had designed for us to excel in. A better way would be for each of God's creatures to develop his or her own gifts while at the same time learning to respect the gifts of others.

God isn't into making clones; we are not the same. He never intended for us to be. God placed each of us in His family with a certain mixture of gifts, temperaments, capabilities, and with every variation in between! When operating in our role and realm of gifting, we will have a greater tendency to excel. We will add tremendous benefit to the body of Christ, and we will experience an incredible joy!

In order to accomplish what God has intended for us, we must do church as a team. A 99% involvement is still 1% shy! We need all of us functioning in our gifts, with respect and love for each other. That's what the church is all about. No one is unimportant. Everyone is a part of the Gospel. Not just the pastor. We do church as a team!

Booker T. Washington, the most influential black leader and educator of his time in America once said, "No race can prosper till it learns that there is as much dignity in tilling a field as in writing a poem." If I understand correctly what he is saying, it is this: every single person is incredibly important to the plan of God being fulfilled! Take hold of that! No one is unimportant. Let that truth burn within your soul. The ministry belongs to you and it *requires* you and me to be involved. It is not the responsibility of a few professional clergy and talented staff people.

The more each one of us takes "ownership" in the ministry of the church, the stronger it becomes! This is really what determines the strength of any church. It is not found in the size of the building, the number of attendees, or the size of its budget. It is the sense of ownership that we as individuals take. It is only when we realize that God has called every single one of us with an equally divine calling that the church will move towards its fullest potential.

So relax! Enjoy who God created you to be! Rest in and cultivate your gifts and God given capabilities. Don't compare yourself with others, and don't be worried about what you don't have. Instead, put to use what you DO have!

There's plenty of room for every creature, every gift, and every style.

Watching it All Come Together

I think the first time I really saw this all come together was at one of our Christmas Eve services in 1996. We had a packed program filled with multi-media, dance, mime, drama, a one-hundred-voice choir, and ensembles; I mean, the works! The auditorium was filled with over twelve hundred people, many who had come for their very first time. I stood just off-stage watching everything unfold as the evening transpired. The choir was radiant. Within the first year, over 1,400 had opened their hearts to Christ, and whenever you have a collection of that many new believers, you'll have fire!

The evening's musical erupted with a song of magnificent celebration. The dancers flowed onto the stage expressing the exuberance of the song with cartwheels and twists. Fred Rodie, a former university cheerleader, came bounding across the platform with flips and somersaults. Others were tossed into the air for the finale, and the auditorium broke into applause. (They threw a couple of the girls so high, we haven't heard from them since!)

Then it hit me. As I watched our outstanding keyboardist, Steve Kenny, play the piano with all his heart, I thought to myself, "Steve is preaching the Gospel the best way he knows how ... through his piano!"

Then I watched Clarke Bright playing the drums so excellently, as he always does. People sometimes like to watch him play because they say he plays more with his heart than he does with his drumsticks. I said to myself, "Clarke is preaching the Gospel the best way he knows how ... through his drums!"

Then I looked into the radiant faces of the choir where many lives had recently been transformed by the Lord's grace, and I said to myself, "Those wonderful people are all preaching the Gospel the best way they know how ... through their singing!" I watched the mime, then the drama, then an ensemble, and I remember thinking, "They're all preaching the Gospel the best way they know how ... through their gifts."

I looked out into the audience to where our video people were running the cameras. I watched the stage coordinators move with such poise and rhythm, rearranging microphones and straightening cords. I observed the ushers greeting people with genuine enthusiasm. I caught the faces of different individuals who had, through their relationships and contacts, invited friends and neighbors. They were all preaching the Gospel through their gifts and passions, talents and contacts. At the end of a most memorable program, I walked out onto the platform, picked up a microphone, and wrapped up the evening with a simple presentation of the Gospel.

And then it dawned on me. I, too, was preaching the Gospel the best way I knew how ... through a microphone. But I wasn't doing it alone. We were doing it together! We were all preaching the Gospel the best way we knew how ... through our gifts! The ushers, the video team, the inviters, greeters, children's workers, parking team, and the rest. Everyone was preaching the best way they knew how! Every single person had a part. It was not one presentation of the Gospel, but over three hundred volunteers contributing their presentations of the Gospel, all at the same time in one evening! That's what made it so powerful!

Then all the pieces began to converge into my mind. I started to see it clearly, and I was flooded with a whole new understanding of how beautiful the Body of Christ can be!

We were doing church as a team! X

CHAPTER THREE STUDY GUIDE
"The Gifts—Commissioned Beyond Ourselves"

1. Each Christian has at least one spiritual gift. Look up the following scriptures. What does each one tell us about the gifts?

    a. 1 Cor. 12:1

    b. Rom. 12:6-8

    c. 1 Cor. 12:4, 8-11

    d. Eph. 4:7-12

2. Why do you think the issue over spiritual gifts has divided the church so much?

3. What is your understanding of how the gifts should operate together in any one church? Should they be segregated? Why or why not?

4. What are your spiritual gifts? List them below as best as you can tell.

5. With your gifts in mind, what possible ministries would you fit well in?

6. If you could do any ministry at all in the church that would make it like "Christmas everyday" for you, which one would that be?

CHAPTER FOUR

Finding Your Fit

Finding Your Fit

"Everyone is a perfect 10 ... somewhere!"

How do we find our place in God's plan? Will it come easily? Where do we start? Each of us is like a piece of a jigsaw puzzle, and every piece has its place. No one piece is optional. How frustrating it would be to attempt putting together a 3,000 piece puzzle only to find one of the pieces missing in the end! That's how God sees us. Every one of us is like a piece of a divine puzzle, and each piece is incredibly important! Everyone is necessary. When all the pieces fit together, people can see a beautiful, completed picture of the heart of Jesus for the world.

You see, everyone is a 10 ... somewhere!

But like a puzzle, each piece doesn't smoothly fall into place on the first attempt. It usually takes repeated tries in order to find the right fit. You turn the piece, try a few others first, and then you try it again. If it doesn't fit on the first go-around, you don't get frustrated and toss the rebellious piece into the trash! No, you keep at it because you know every piece is a perfect 10 ... somewhere!

"But I am just one piece," you might rationalize. "They can do without me. Why, there's 2,999 other pieces. I'm just one, insignificant piece. They'll never miss me."

Don't you dare think that way. In fact, that's exactly the way the enemy of our souls would love for you to think. But don't you do it even for a minute. If God didn't have a place for you, He wouldn't have had you born! But He did, therefore, you are incredibly important to His plan being accomplished!

Breaking Through Limitations

Each of us knows what it means to be sentenced to limitations we and others place on our lives. It could come through our upbringing, past circumstances, parent's comments, from friends or even from our own failures. These mental "ceilings" restrain us from discovering our fullest potential. But God's power is available to each and every one of us. He is able even when we are not. He is strong when we are weak, and regardless of how we feel, God will always find a way! If we are going to become what God has designed us to become, we must discover these "false ceilings" in our life and break through them to new levels!

Have you ever been to a circus and seen one of those huge multi-ton elephants? Their strength is incredible. I remember going to a circus and I saw one of these elephants outside the big top, so in my innocent way, I crawled under the rope to get a closer look. I was shocked to notice that as strong as these animals were, this monstrous pachyderm was kept under control by a tiny rope attached to a foot long stake in the dirt! It would wander to the full length of the rope, and when it felt a little tug, it would stop. Why with one flick of its huge foot, that elephant could have sent that stake flying through the air... with the greatest of ease!

Later on, I asked one of the caretakers about this inconsistency. He explained to me that as a young elephant, they would tie it up to a very strong stake. After pulling and tugging on it to no avail, the elephant figures that getting loose would be a hopeless attempt. So it relinquishes itself to no longer trying. Then when the elephant grows up (and gets bigger!) it still has this limitation in its mind. Now all the caretaker has to do is to put a little stake in the ground, attach a flimsy rope to its foot, and it won't go anywhere. Why? Because it doesn't believe that it can! It has been conditioned to think small!

How much potential do you have, and how willing are you to reach for God's fullest measure? In fact, let's take a look at your potential for a moment. Your potential is like an iceberg that is 1/10th above the water with the other 9/10th under the surface. Your potential is the whole iceberg, but most of us use only the 1/10th above the water. With God's help, you can turn that potential into its fullest use for the Lord!

In the following questions, rate yourself as to how much of your potential you estimate that you are reaching. Put a percentage in the space next to each category. How do you fare?

1. Spiritual Growth   _____

2. Personal Growth   _____

3. Financial Health   _____

4. People Skills   _____

5. Physical Health   _____

6. Vocational Abilities   _____

7. Family Health   _____

8. As A Leader in Church   _____

9. Relationship with Friends _____

Finding Your D.E.S.I.G.N.

Every person is absolutely unique in his or her design, and God doesn't want you to settle for anything less than His very best! You are created with special talents, abilities and gifts. That's wonderful in itself, but what's even more important is how you invest those characteristics! We must discover and develop them to their fullest potential! It is only then that we will be able to crash through barriers of limitation.

There are many wonderful courses you can take to find your gifts and passions. One of the ways we determine our gift mix is through New Hope's DESIGN course. It is taught twice a year at our "Doing Church as a Team" conferences. The more you understand the way He designed you to be, the better you can cooperate with that design! There is no guarantee that a person's gifts will be accurately pinpointed upon graduation, but I do guarantee that there will be a much greater appreciation and understanding of gifts!

Creighton Arita, who oversees the DESIGN course, came up with its name. It is an acrostic that stands for the different ingredients that when they're combined, it equals ... "you." When you recognize and develop each of these six categories, you'll be on your way to realizing your full potential in Christ!

Here's what the acrostic stands for:

D ... Desire

This identifies your passion. If all things were equal and you could do anything in the world for the Lord, what would that be to make it feel like Christmas everyday? Did you know that God placed certain desires in you as one of His ways of telling you what He wants you to do? He not only gives you certain abilities, but He will even give you the "desire" to accompany what He's asked you to do! Philippians 2:13 tells us that "It is God who is at work within us to both *will* and to *do* His good pleasure!" Isn't that incredible? I think so!

E ... Experience

Your past experiences are important considerations in finding your design. What tasks or projects in the past that influenced you over the years? Even the negative experiences, God will use as part of your design. What have you learned from them? How have they made you more compassionate towards other in the same situations?

God will never waste a hurt. In fact, one of my favorite verses is Psalms 56:8 that says, "Thou hast taken account of my wanderings; put my tears in Thy bottle; are they not in Thy book?"

God has put all your tears in a bottle. In other words, He remembers them all and will use them for your good. Some people think that due to their past or the way they were raised, it is impossible for them to succeed. Consider these examples of great people who had to overcome past obstacles:

He didn't talk till he was four years old and he didn't start to read till he was seven. One of his teachers labeled him as "mentally slow, unsociable and adrift in his foolish dreams." This is what was often said of Albert Einstein.

"He's too stupid to learn anything," said some of the teachers of a young boy named Thomas Edison.

"He possesses minimal football knowledge and lacks motivation," an expert said of a beginning coach named Vince Lombardi.

He went bankrupt several times and was fired by the editor of a local newspaper because he apparently had a "lack of ideas." The man they fired was Walt Disney.

He failed the sixth grade and had a lifetime of setbacks and defeats. Finally as a senior citizen, Winston Churchill became the Prime Minister of England.

S ... Spiritual Gift

Every person who knows Jesus Christ is endowed with one or more spiritual gifts. These are enumerated in 1 Corinthians 12, Romans 12, Ephesians 4, and in 1 Peter 4. God never intended for His ministry to cease when He ascended into heaven, so He decided that His ministry would be carried on through Believers. Knowing that we could never do it on our own, He distributed gifts to His Church through which He would carry on His work. What are your spiritual gifts? Are you willing for God to use you in any of them?

I ... Individual Style

Each of us has a unique temperament that we call that our individual style. Some of us are more extroverted and some tend towards being more introverted. We all know of individuals who are obviously "people persons" while others are more "task oriented." Some are very structured and others are impetuously spontaneous and unstructured. Your individual style is all part of your design. The more you understand the way God created you, the better you can cooperate with it.

Your style will tell you "how" you carry out your calling as a Christian. It will not change your calling. Each of us must run the race set before us. We may each do it *differently*, but the main thing is that we run the race!

I have never been a salesman. I remember when I was supposed to sell tickets for a school project; I would beg my dad to buy them all so I wouldn't have to sell them door to door. Once, I took all the money I had saved to pay for a box of almond chocolates our school was selling. Twenty-five bars at a dollar per bar! Later, I gave them away as gifts.

I remember when I became a Christian in college. I attended a course in evangelism held by Campus Crusade for Christ. Now this is an outstanding Christian group founded by Bill Bright. They perfected the "Four Spiritual Laws," a little booklet used to win many to Christ. We took a whole morning class on how to use this booklet, and then came the moment of truth. The final project was that we were to go door to door and share the Four Spiritual Laws for the last two hours! I almost died! All the other students seemed so excited, and I felt like such a worm because I didn't want to win anyone to the Lord!

While everyone else was zealously banging on doors, I quietly found a McDonald's nearby, read my Bible for two hours and repented that I couldn't lead anyone to the Lord. When everyone returned with glowing reports, I just sat there in the corner of the room hoping no one would notice me. I felt guilty and condemned, unworthy to even be called a Christian!

On the other hand, I love the arts. I love music, creative presentations with multi-media, story telling, and song writing. Over the years, I've pursued these with a passion. In Bible College, I formed a musical group that traveled throughout the country each summer singing and speaking at dozens of youth camps. Through the use of the arts and through public speaking, I have seen hundreds of people come to Christ. During the first year of our recent pioneer venture of New Hope Oahu, I was humbled to find out that God had allowed me to be a small part of seeing over 1,800 receive Christ for the first time! That is equivalent to five people a day being won to Christ! My calling is still the same although my design will dictate the style that I am most comfortable with.

G ... Growth Phase

Each of us is still growing in the Lord. Some of us may be like spiritual toddlers, others like adolescents or adults. Some have knowledge but have a long way to go in wisdom; i.e. the applying of that knowledge to every day living. Others have great common sense but know very little of the Bible.

There's a common misnomer that spiritual growth is measured by time spent in the church or by a person's length of stay. The truth of the matter is that in one or two years, a person who is intent on following the Lord can be much more mature with insight and wisdom than another Christian who after ten years simply cruises along without much involvement. We have to remember that Jesus turned over the responsibility for administrating the whole Church to former fishermen and tax gatherers who were just 3 ½ years old in the Lord! Christian growth is more measured by a person's willingness to apply what he has heard than it is by length of stay in the church. John 13:17 reminds us, "If you know these things, you are blessed if you **do** them" (emphasis mine).

Are you an infant, toddler, adolescent, young adult, or mature adult in your relationship with Christ? Your growth phase is factored as part of your "design."

N ... Natural Abilities

All of us have seen "natural athletes" who seem to excel in any sport they dive into. People have natural abilities in other areas as well, whether it is in computers, working with children, mechanics, electronics, or problem solving. Our natural abilities are an important component in who God made us to be.

What do you enjoy doing? Do you have a natural talent in fixing things? What about strategic planning, financial planning, working with the elderly or working with babies? When we work with our design, life gets exciting and fun. You see, God isn't some unbending drillmaster who demands your service. He really wants your heart! In fact it is so important that He tells us in Deuteronomy 28:47, "Because you did not serve the Lord your God with joy and a glad heart for the abundance of all things, therefore you shall serve your enemies..." You see, God wants us not just to serve Him. He wants us to serve Him with a joyful and a glad heart! Then you'll be functioning in the way God designed you to function!

Add all these together and you'll find your DESIGN. These ingredients help you to find the shape and placement of your puzzle piece. Now all you need to add to this recipe is involvement!

Patience: the Breakfast of Champions

Finding your fit may take time. Be patient. God may want to build character quality before He fits us into our niche! But in either case, be patient. Everything has an order to it, and we can't push our way into God's plan.

When you start on a puzzle, the first thing that usually happens is that the edge pieces are fit together, forming sort of a frame. These are usually easier to assemble because one of the sides will have a straight edge to it. Then you start working your way towards the middle.

Finding your fit in the church may have many similarities. Like fitting the pieces of a puzzle together, it requires patience! Sometimes, you'll see others getting assimilated almost immediately! When that happens, there will be a tendency to accuse them of being part of the "in-crowd" while you struggle with feeling like an outsider.

But relax! Like the inner pieces of a puzzle, you'll need to be patient. You may not be able to find your fit until two or three other edge pieces find theirs first. Then, lo and behold, you might very well be that piece which joins them all together! So don't give up even if you think that you're just one measly, unimportant piece. You'd be surprised at the power of just one! You can make a huge difference! Everybody's a 10 ... somewhere!

Here is an excerpt taken from a speech by John Salisbury given on the radio in Portland, Oregon some years ago. It is titled "One Vote."

In 1776, one vote gave America the English language instead of the German.

In 1845, one vote brought Texas into the Union.

In 1868, one vote saved President Andrew Johnson from being impeached.

In 1876, one vote gave Rutherford B. Hayes the U. S. Presidency.

In 1923, one vote gave Adolph Hitler control of the Nazi party.

You are just one, but you count!

Three Results of Using Your Gifts

God designed us to be intricately involved in His plan. When you are willing to launch out and use your gifts for the sake of the Kingdom, three things will begin to happen.

An Amazing Joy!

You will experience an amazing joy when you are operating in your gift. In fact, the Greek word for spiritual gifts is *charismaton*. The prefix is the word *charis* or grace. The root word of grace? It is the word "*char*" which means, "joy"! Yes, joy is at the very root of using your spiritual gift.

In his book, *The Anatomy of an Illness*, Norman Cousins relates an instructive story of Pablo Casals, one of the great musicians of the 20th century. It is a story of belief and renewal that we all can learn from. Cousins describes

Casals on his 90th birthday. His arthritis and frailty were so debilitating that it was almost unbearable to watch him begin his day.

His emphysema was evident in his labored breathing. He walked with a shuffle, stooped over with his head pitched forward. His hands were swollen, his fingers clenched, and he looked like a very tired, old man. But even before eating breakfast Pablo Casals would make his way to the piano, one of the instruments on which he had become very proficient. Laboriously and with great difficulty, he arranged himself on the piano bench. It seemed like such a terrible effort for him to bring his clenched, swollen fingers even to the keyboard.

Then something miraculous happened. Casals began to be completely transformed. As he played an instrument that he so loved, moving in where he was so gifted, his physiology changed and produced in his body as well as on the piano, a result that should have only come from a strong, healthy person. His fingers slowly unlocked and reached toward the keys like the buds of a plant reach toward the sunlight. He began with a rendition of Bach, then onto a Brahms concerto as his fingers raced across the keyboard. His whole body seemed to be fused with the music. It was no longer stiff and shrunken but graceful and completely freed from the arthritic bondage.

By the time he walked away from the piano, he seemed an entirely different person from the one that sat down in the first place. He stood taller and walked without a trace of a shuffle. He immediately moved to the breakfast table, ate a hearty meal, then went out for a stroll along the beach!

Isn't that wonderful! It is so graphic in illustrating how God designed us to function in our gifts! When we do, we feel better!

A Healthy Accountability

If you are a solo artist, you don't need accountability. You don't need to keep rhythm with anyone else. You're it! You're the big cheese! But when you start using your gifts and doing church as a team, you will need to match your stroke to the others. You will need to show up when you are scheduled to. You will need to hang in there when the going gets tough. You won't be allowed to just quit when the winds pick up. You'll be required to be accountable!

But why is accountability so important? Without accountability, we will never build character. Accountability is one of God's favorite tools. Watch those who have chosen to dodge accountability. They look good in the calm, but when the storms hit, they usually are no match for the stresses and currents. It won't be long before they capsize. Character is the inner strength that takes you to the finish. It's the weight in our lives, and accountability is our "weight trainer."

Without accountability, we will never build character.

Michael Plant was one of the world's best yachtsmen. He navigated the Pacific as well as the Atlantic as a solo voyager numerous times. Through those experiences, he gained skill and notoriety.

In 1992, he decided to go all the way. He purchased a state-of-the-art sailboat with the best navigational equipment money could buy. His dreamboat was christened, "The Coyote."

On this state-of-the-art sailboat was an emergency locating indicator system much like that of a transponder. With one press of a button, it would send out a signal that would be picked up by satellite. Within ten seconds, either of two ground locations could pinpoint his coordinates anywhere in the middle of the ocean. It was the most fail-safe vessel of its kind.

Early in the fall of 1992, Michael Plant decided to set out from the East Coast on a solo voyage in the Coyote, destination France. On the fourth day into the voyage, the ground locators lost contact with the Coyote. However, when checking the weather scans of the Atlantic, it was found that storms were causing high seas. They concluded that Michael Plant was simply navigating the storms and would soon regain contact. But he never did.

Search and Rescue squads were deployed to comb the trail of the Coyote, but to no avail. Commercial airliners were asked to monitor their emergency channels in case he tried sending out signals for help.

Around the fifteenth day after his departure, a ship about 400 miles off the Azores came upon the Coyote, floating upside down. If there's one position a state-of-the-art sailboat will not be found in, it's upside down.

Hoisting the Coyote up for a closer look, they searched the cabin hoping to find the emergency life raft already deployed indicating that Michael Plant would be floating somewhere in the Atlantic. But instead of a missing life raft, they found it only partially inflated, still stuck in the hull of the boat. Until this day, the body of Michael Plant has never been found.

But the tell tale culprit was a broken keel. No one knows whether the Coyote hit some ocean sewage, a submarine, or a whale, but the ballast was broken off leaving the Coyote without any weight in the keel. The ballast was an 8,000-pound weight placed in the keel making this sailboat one of the safest vessels on the ocean. Because of the amount of weight in the keel, even should it capsize, the design of the ballast would roll it upright again. Yet without the weight in the keel, the Coyote became no match for the storms of the Atlantic.

I don't know much about sailing, but this one thing I do know. To have stability in the storms, there must be *more weight beneath the water line than above it*. Without the ballast, the Coyote could look fine in the bay or in calm water. It could have its sails unfurled and colors flying, but without any weight in its keel, it would be unable to launch any further into the deep. One person said it this way: "Ships are safe in the harbor, but that's not what ships were made for."

Our character is the "weight beneath the water line." Without it, we may look good in the harbor. We could fly our colors and strut our stuff, but we would be no match for the currents. Storms alone don't develop character. They may reveal it, but only *genuine accountability will build it.*

An Accelerated Growth

God designed us to use our gifts. We were created to serve, anointed to serve, and gifted to serve. That's God's plan. In fact, using our gifts to serve is a crucial and indispensable ingredient for our spiritual growth. It's all a part of the package.

Last year, we took a tour to Israel. One of my favorite stops was at the Dead Sea. It's a beautiful, expansive lake touching Jordan's borders on its eastern shore and Israel in the west. The mineral deposits of the Dead Sea are abundant making it one of the richest spots on the face of the earth. Normal ocean water contains about 4% mineral content giving it the "salty" taste. The Dead Sea has a mineral content of 22%! Scattered throughout the lake you can see pillars of salt, or rather minerals that stand like stalagmites, reaching toward the surface like lone soldiers waiting for a command. The water, which resembles more baby oil than it does ocean water, lazily laps the shores.

However, as beautiful and as rich as the Dead Sea is, you won't see any of the familiar sites usually seen around middle eastern lakes. No fishing villages, no boats, no drying nets, no haggling over fish prices or sea gulls gliding overhead. Why?

Because nothing lives in the Dead Sea; hence, its name. The heavy mineral content makes it unlivable for fish or any other living creatures common to nearby lakes such as the Sea of Galilee. The Dead Sea is rich, but dead. Abundant and wealthy, but lifeless.

The main reason for the absence of teeming schools of fish is because there is no outlet. For eons, the headwaters of the Jordan have fed this lake, freely depositing her mineral treasures found along the way. But because the Dead Sea cul-de-sacs into a desert that's nearly 1,000 feet below sea level, it releases its intake of water only through evaporation. There is no other outlet. There are no currents of water, no flowing tributaries, and no life to embrace within its shores.

Churches can turn into Dead Seas, rich in content but lifeless. There is only one way to begin the life process flowing, and that's to open up an outlet! We've got to get our gifts moving and our hearts serving, and then the currents of life will reappear. Every church runs the risk of entropy and stagnation. It can look good from afar, but like the fig tree, it may be scarce in fruit up close! Using our gifts to do church as a team is a nonnegotiable part of growth.

People are like sponges. If a sponge is put under a faucet of running water, it soon becomes saturated. Once that happens, you can run the water over it all day, but it won't be able to absorb any more water. The only way to restore its absorbency is to wring it out!

As Christians, we absorb teaching, instruction, God's Word and His promises, but at some point along the way, we will stop growing. We get saturated, and our capacity to absorb diminishes. Then no matter how many more messages we hear, we'll cease being able to absorb any more until we wring out our sponges. Then, and only then, will our absorbency return.

Wring out your sponge and serve! Don't hang on to the water! Give it freely away. There's plenty where that came from!

When I was in high school, I was a novice at playing the guitar. I would add about one new chord a month to my repertoire of musical knowledge. It was a slow boat to guitar proficiency, but I figured that "slow and steady" was better than not having launched at all. I would dream about being in a band, playing guitar for our school dances, proms, and other activities, but according to my present pace, I calculated that it would take me another 170 years before I'd be ready.

Well, my big chance came at the end of my junior year. Just before summer began, the lead guitarist of the best band in our school approached me. They were looking for a rhythm guitarist and lead vocalist. He asked if I would consider joining up with them. I was flabbergasted! It was my dream come true. Of course I said yes!

Only one catch. The summer schedule of the band would commence in three weeks, and I had to learn twenty new songs. We would hold practice three times a week until we got the new songs down.

I was so excited, I couldn't sleep at night! I would sing those songs over and over until I had memorized every word, every move, and every chord. Each waking moment was dedicated to learning. I can't even remember whether or not I passed my finals that year. I guess I did. Anyway, one thing I do remember. When I wasn't playing in a band, my growth curve on the guitar was minimal at best! But as soon as I got involved, my growth accelerated at least 200 percent! I learned chords I didn't even know existed! I had boundless energy and would look forward to every chance at playing guitar.

Getting involved by using your gifts accelerates your spiritual growth immensely! God designed us that way. Don't head for the grandstands when you enter the Kingdom of God. Head for the playing field. That's where the excitement is. That's where the action is.

But most of all, that's where our Coach is!

The Fastest Way to the Throne

"But when you are invited, go and recline at the last place, so that when the one who has invited you comes, he may say to you, 'Friend, move up higher'; then you will have honor in the sight of all who are at the table with you. For everyone who exalts himself shall be humbled, and he who humbles himself shall be exalted" (Luke 14:10-11).

Allow me to address the heart of a servant. Regardless of a person's gifts, talents, or abilities, each of us is called to the foot of the table. That's more a matter of the heart than it is a matter of giftedness. One of our favorite sayings is, "The fastest way to the Throne will always be through the servant's entry." Jesus models servanthood to us, and when we develop our gifts, we begin by entering through the servant's entry. It constantly reminds us of the heart behind serving. Entering through the servant's entry means being willing to start at the foot of the table. Whatever the need is, we get to be willing to pick up a towel and wash someone's feet.

Using your gifts in the church is not always a guarantee that God will bless you. It needs to be used with the right heart and with the right motives. Sometimes people use gifts to "justify" their behavior. If there's a job that is disliked, a person may say, "Oh that just isn't my gift. That's not my passion." When that happens, it is not an issue of gifts or passion. Rather, it is an issue of the heart. Your gifts and passion may identify your style of ministry, but it does not excuse or justify it.

There is an incredible tendency in each of us to use religious cloaks to justify selfish motives. It's nothing new. All our lives, the arrows of attention and interest were turned inward, and some of those arrows are difficult to redirect. Turning them outward takes daily effort and a constant commitment to purity and servant-heartedness.

The late Mother Teresa of the Sisters of Charity has spoken to my heart through her books over the years. She has exemplified to me the untiring heart of a servant. She was an incredible leader who modeled what it meant to serve. In the classic book, *The Love of Christ*, edited by George Gorree and Jean Barbier, Mother Teresa writes of her magnificent work in Calcutta. She reflects in an interview:

> *"What we are doing is but a drop in the ocean. This may be only a drop, but the ocean would be less if it weren't there. What we do is something small, but we do it with big hearts. At death, we will not be judged by the amount of work we did, but by the amount of love we put into it. We do not strive for spectacular actions. What counts is the gift of yourself, the degree of love you put into each of your deeds ... Do you want to be great? Pick up a broom and sweep the floor."*

I love that. She exemplifies for me the heart of a servant that God used to touch a needy world. She was content to serve an "Audience of One," as Greg Ferguson so aptly composed. She didn't clean tables with a wash cloth. She cleaned them with her heart. She didn't give speeches with eloquence. She gave them with her heart.

When you serve, serve with your heart. Whether you teach, sing, pass out bulletins, play an instrument, set up chairs, or clean tables, always remember that it is not the size of the task, but the size of the heart you put into the task that makes what you do something beautiful for God!

God Deserves Our Best

One of New Hope's core values is that God is worthy of our very best. We have coined a saying around the church: "Simplicity with Excellence." Because of the fact that whatever we do is for an audience of One, everything matters! Whether we're cleaning a table or rolling up a microphone cord, God does not deserve our leftovers. He deserves the best we can give!

Excellence is very different from perfection or opulence. That is not what the Lord expects. A spirit of excellence is a quality found in Daniel's life (Dan. 5:12). A spirit of excellence is a constant desire to give our first fruits; our very best in all we do because we are serving the King of Kings!

Some months ago, a clothing store called me up and asked if I would come and pick up a few boxes. They wanted to donate them to a worthy cause, such as a church. They said that one of the bosses from the corporate headquarters was coming in, and they needed to "spruce" up the place. The boxes were in the way.

Mark Hovland, our Director of Care Ministries, and I had just been talking about setting up a "thrift store" in our church, so the invitation to pick up some items from a clothing outlet excited me. Maybe they'd have enough clothing to get the thrift store started!

When I arrived at the store, the manager had me load two large boxes into my car. I didn't even ask what the contents were. Grateful for the donation, I simply thanked him and left.

As soon as I arrived home, I opened the boxes to see what might be the beginnings of our new ministry. To my surprise, the boxes contained nothing I had expected. They were filled with broken, soiled, or returned items that the store deemed "beyond repair."

Broken purses, mismatched earrings, torn clothing, pants that had broken zippers, sunglasses that were scratched and other unusable pieces of apparel made up the contents of the two-boxed donations. My heart sank! Every item had been returned to the store due to some defect. They had thrown these items into the boxes. Now that they were full, the management needed to dispose of them. These items would go either to the dump or to the church. This time, I guess the church won.

I did what I could to repair the items that were repairable and disposed of the rest. Two days later, I was further amused when the manager called me and asked for a tax-deductible receipt!

After musing over these things, I came to an even more gripping realization. "Where did they learn this? Who taught them that if they had a choice between trashing something or giving it to God, that it would be a nice, benevolent thing to at least let God have it?"

We have taught them those lessons! Over the years, we as Christians have modeled that quite well! If there were old sweaters with holes in them, pants that didn't fit, or things we couldn't use anymore, it was time to give those things to the church!

God deserves the very first of our hearts not our last. When you worship, worship with everything that is in you! If you serve, serve Him with all you've got. If you should sing, sing your heart out! Train, don't just try. Prepare, don't just perform. Practice, don't just pray. Do both, and in doing so, you will be giving God your best! Everything matters because He deserves our everything! ✗

CHAPTER FOUR STUDY GUIDE

"Finding Your Fit"

1. Using the acrostic, DESIGN, list personal characteristics that would best identify you.

    Desire:

    Experience:

    Spiritual Gift:

    Individual Style:

    Growth Phase:

    Natural Abilities:

2. Why do you think accountability is so difficult for some people?

3. What would the hardest tests of accountability be for you?

4. Read Daniel 5:12. Daniel is said to have possessed an "extraordinary spirit." Some versions have it listed as a "spirit of excellence." What would some of the characteristics be of this kind of spirit?

Mining Out Leadership Gifts in the Church

Chapter Five

Mining Out Leadership Gifts in the Church

"I have a dream!"—Martin Luther King, Jr.

Dream Releasers

I lived in Japan during my junior high school years. My father served in the Army. For three years, he was stationed in a small town called Zama. It was a beautiful place, but it was still an Army installation enclosed by barbed wire. The inside looked like any old American town, but outside the fences held the mystique of Japan. I used to look forward to our trips off base and into the countryside.

One summer day, all of us kids jumped into the car for a ride into the cool mountains surrounding Tokyo. We stopped at a lookout point that offered us a breathtaking view of one of the lush valleys beneath. It was a beautiful sight. The mountains were blanketed with cedar trees. The valleys below stretched out as far as you could see, each one reaching out to the sleepy village.

We decided to stop for lunch. On one side, a little Japanese woman was selling *bentos*, Japanese box lunches. On the other side, a man dressed in a traditional *yukatta* or "happy coat" with *getta* sandals caught my attention. He was selling tiny birds. He held ten or so bamboo cages, each one containing a small bird that resembled a finch.

"Irrashai-mase!" he called. "Welcome! May I help you?"

"How much for one bird?" I asked.

"100 yen each," he called back in Japanese.

In those days, 100 yen was worth about 36 cents, so I thought for such a deal, I'd take one! I handed the vendor a 100 yen coin, and in exchange, I chose one of the bamboo cages containing a tiny finch.

As I began to walk back toward the car to show off my new purchase, he called out after me.

"Sumimasen!" (Excuse me!) "Don't forget to bring the cage back when you're done!"

"Bring back the cage when I'm done?" I questioned. "I'm not planning to eat the thing. I just want to take it home as a pet."

"Oh, no," he replied. "You don't understand! The bird and the cage are not for you to take home. The 100 yen is to take the bird to the edge of the valley and release it so it will be able to fly freely!"

Quite frankly, that was about the last thing in the world I had on my mind. Release the bird that I had just bought with my hard-earned money? That was ridiculous!

That sounded like the dumbest thing I had ever heard of. But I didn't have a choice. The man was keeping a close watch on me to make sure he retrieved his cage.

I guess the more I thought about it, the more novel it sounded. Why not? I figured it was worth a try! So, I walked over to the edge of the ravine overlooking the valley below. I opened the cage door, and gave the bird a couple of nudges. He edged his way suspiciously toward the door of the cage, and then launched into flight with a jubilant duet of tweets and whistles. I watched the bird fly over the valley, swirl his way back towards me as if to respectfully say, "thank you." Then he soared so high that I lost him in the sun. Within moments, he had disappeared.

I returned the cage to the vendor who bowed in the gracious Japanese form. I didn't return home with a bird, but I did with something much greater: a profound lesson that has been with me ever since, forever changing my perspective about serving people. Looking back on it now, I would have paid 100 times more if I knew how profound that one experience would be to me years later. I learned the precious lesson of being a "dream releaser."

"Tell 'Em I Died Rich!"

The story is told of two miners who spent half their lives looking for gold in the Pacific Northwest. Amidst the scrutiny and criticism of the townspeople, the two miners pressed on believing in their ability to strike it rich. These two unrelenting miners became the joke of the town, as they would return empty-handed week after week. Nevertheless, they pressed on with a deep confidence that someday they would find what they were looking for.

One sultry afternoon, after months of painstaking digging into an old mine shaft, they finally struck it rich! Huge nuggets of gold were chipped out of a rich, undiscovered vein. Furiously, the men began pulling nugget after nugget from the grip of the earth.

No one knows whether it was a faulty support pole, the exuberance of their shouts, or the gradual loosening of the dirt, but the sound of loud, piercing cracks suddenly brought them to an abrupt halt. Within moments, the mineshaft began caving in. At the first shock, tons of ceiling dirt pounded both men to the floor of the shaft. One of the men lay injured on the ground, holding tightly to a nugget he had claimed.

"Come on!" yelled the first miner. "We've got to get out of here before the whole thing collapses! I'll help you! Get up! Leave the gold. We don't have a second to lose!"

The injured miner, still clutching the gold nugget tightly to his chest replied, "No. Just leave me here. I found what I've been looking for. I've spent my life searching for this vein, and I'm not about to let it go now! Leave me here. You go! Get out of here."

"Don't be foolish! We've gotta' get you back!" the first replied. Just then, another quake hit the rafters spilling more dirt into the already dust-filled shaft.

"If I leave you here, you'll surely die! What will I tell your family! What will I tell the folks back in town?"

The injured miner wheezed his final words between strained coughs as dust filled the collapsing chamber.

"Just tell 'em I died rich," he whispered with a final breath. "Just tell 'em I died rich!"

Too Many Are Dying Rich

The church is laden with treasures, dreams and precious gifts, and too many are going to their graves with songs left unsung, gifts yet unwrapped, and dreams yet unreleased. Too many are dying rich! Like the bird in Japan, these treasures and dreams need to be released. In every person's heart is a dream of what he or she can become for the Lord; a dream that sees them making a difference in the world, in their families, in their churches.

God calls every leader to be a dream releaser. There is nothing more spectacular than seeing people's dreams released and being used for the glory of God! There's just no greater joy!

That's what Loren Cunningham did in Youth With A Mission. The dreams that were in thousands of young people's hearts to go into the mission fields were released and brought to pass. Through his vision and leadership, Loren mobilized scores of young evangelists who are still bringing the Good News to unreached people groups today.

Mother Teresa did that in Calcutta. God had deposited the gift of mercy and servanthood into the hearts of thousands of willing servants. However, before Mother Teresa entered the scene, those gifts lay dormant. She found a way for those dreams to be discovered, developed, and deployed in reaching the poorest of the poor in Calcutta.

Each of us has dreams in our hearts just waiting to be released. These gifts, if mobilized and aligned toward a common, God-glorifying purpose, can transform any church into a powerful army for the Lord.

Building a Leadership Base

May I offer a word to pastors and leaders? One of the most critical keys to doing church as a team is building an ever-increasing core of servant-leaders. You were not designed to do it alone. You are not a one-man band. No one is. It's no fun being a one-man band, but doing church as a team is!

Let me illustrate it this way. Imagine that I held out before you a one-foot square piece of cardboard and onto it, I emptied a bucket of white sand. The sand would accumulate, and as it did, a pyramid of sand would form. Now, what if would happen if I poured another bucket of sand onto it? It would increase the amount of sand on the cardboard until it could hold no more. Then what would happen to the excess sand? That's right. It would overflow the edges and cascade onto the floor beneath. The cardboard base could only hold so much. Now, what if I emptied, not just another bucket ... but a barrel of sand onto it? Would it hold any more? Obviously not! What would happen? Why, it would overflow the cardboard base and spill onto the floor. Forgive my pressing of the issue, but now what would happen if I emptied a truckload of sand onto it? Would it hold any more? No!

What would I have to do for it to hold more sand? You've got it!

I would have to expand the base!

Leaders in any church can be likened to that piece of cardboard. The larger the base, the more sand it can hold. If the base is small, it doesn't matter how much sand is poured onto it. It will be impossible for it to hold any more sand ... at least not until you increase the base! That's the whole secret to what many churches call, "closing the back door." Some churches feel as if they are like turnstiles where people come in but never stay. These visitors can't seem to get assimilated into the life of the church, so they leave. Increasing the base of leadership, or building a solid core of leaders is primary to any church's foundation for the future.

The first step in building a core of leaders is to believe that they are there! You must believe that God would never call a leader to oversee a ministry without providing everything necessary for its fruitfulness and success! God is not so cruel as to call you to build an ark without providing the necessary materials for its completion!

The same is true with servant-leaders. God will provide all that you need to fulfill what He has called each church to do. But first, you must believe that the leaders are there! Why? Because they are! Look for them. See them. They might be right under your nose, but if you are not looking for them, you'll never see them.

If I am looking for my shoes, but don't believe that they are in the closet, then I won't look there. In the same way, if I don't believe that there are great potential leaders in the church, I won't look there either! I'll have every reason in the world for why things just aren't happening like they should. Reason? "Because we have no leaders!"

God Has Already Provided

In Exodus 15:22-26, we find the first of Israel's many complaints. They crossed the Red Sea and traveled inland until they ran out of water. The hot sands of the Sinai baked the Israelites until they were parched and thirsty. After a few miles, they came upon a small lake, but the water was bitter and unfit to drink. Like the bitterness of the lake, anger, grumbling, and disgust were unleashed toward Moses and Aaron as they cried, "What shall we drink?"

Verse 25 gives us a beautiful gem for every leader. "Then he cried out to the Lord, and the Lord showed him a tree; and he threw it into the waters, and the waters became sweet."

Moses cried out to the Lord, and when he did, God *showed* him a tree. Now re-read this portion again and you will discover that God didn't create a tree, then conveniently arrange for Moses to find it. It had always been there! God just showed him a tree.

Moses and Aaron must have walked by that tree dozens of times without ever realizing its potential! The children of Israel may have eaten lunch under that very same tree! They probably even complained about the bitter water from under that tree.

Why were they complaining? They were complaining because God hadn't provided an answer to their dilemma: the bitter waters. But all the while, their answer was right under their noses! (Or rather, right above their heads.) But because they were too busy complaining about what they didn't have, their eyes were blinded to what they did have! Too preoccupied with what God had not provided, they were oblivious to what He had!

Let God show you the tree. It's there. And so are your leaders. You may be having lunch with them this week! You may be fellowshipping with them, but you won't ever be able to see them until you believe that they are there!

"You Gotta' Believe That They're There!"

A dear pastor friend and I were talking over lunch one day. He was having trouble finding quality leaders. He was on the edge of "burn-out" from undertaking many of the ministry responsibilities by himself.

"If I had a bigger church," he observed, "there would be more leaders to choose from. But, right now there just aren't any!"

My reply to him came in the form of a question. "When you look at a forest, what do you see?" I asked.

"Elementary, Watson!" he quipped. "Trees!"

"That's your problem," I replied. "All you see are trees. You've got to see more than trees. You've got to see the houses!"

I could tell that he wasn't quite tracking with me.

"Let me explain," I continued. "When I look at a forest, I see houses! I see beautiful dressers, rocking chairs, bed frames, cabinets, and desks! They're all in the forest, and they're beautiful!"

From the look on his face, I could tell that he was beginning to re-evaluate our friendship and secretly question the benefit of us ever having lunch together. But before he could come to any premature conclusions, I hastened to my point.

"No, you won't find them already completed. But the potential is all there! Sure, you'll still have to cut and sand the wood. But it's all there! Everything you need is in that forest. You just need to see more than trees in order to be motivated to harvest the wood! You have to see their potential! You have to believe that there's gold in 'them thar hills' in order to muster up the energy necessary to mine it out!"

When you believe that they are there, you'll be surprised how many wonderful leaders start showing up! ✘

CHAPTER FIVE STUDY GUIDE

"Mining Out Leadership Gifts in the Church"

1. List three dreams you have tucked away in your heart that have yet to come true.

   a.

   b.

   c.

2. What factors are hindering each one from coming to pass?

   a.

   b.

   c.

3. What are some of the reasons that hinder us from seeing our own potential?

4. What are some of the reasons that hinder us from seeing other people's potential?

CHAPTER SIX

Developing Servant-Leaders

Developing Servant-Leaders

Look for evidences of God's presence, not evidences of His absence.

———— ⚬ ————

One of the greatest roles of a pastor is to believe in people. This one quality alone can do more to develop emerging leaders than anything else! We all need someone to believe in us, see the best in us, and help us to bring it forth! Sure, there may be many faults still needing to be corrected, but what we need are people who will see beyond our glitches to God's best.

In Mark 2, we find a story about Jesus seeing the best in people. He calls it "faith."

The story opens with the four zealous friends of a paralytic man whom we'll call Reuben. They had recently heard talk of a carpenter from Nazareth. Reports had it that this Jesus would be teaching at Peter's house in Capernaum. Now, a visiting dignitary was not necessarily a unique occasion. They would often entertain guest Rabbis in the neighborhood synagogues, but what caught their attention was the part about Him being able to heal hurting people! Maybe He could heal Reuben!

That evening with their friend on a stretcher, they began the journey to Peter's house. However, the weight and awkwardness of the load delayed their arrival. By the time they reached the home, a crowd had filled the living room and overflowed into the back yard, leaving no room for late comers, let alone Reuben and his friends.

Refusing to have their hopes dashed, the most creative among them came up with a risky idea.

"I know what we can do!" he said. "Let's climb up on the roof and make a hole! You heard me. Make a hole! Then we can let him down on the stretcher right in front of Jesus! That'll get His attention, won't it? That should get Him to notice Reuben!"

Whether there was no time to consult with Reuben or they simply chose not to, the story does not disclose. But, we do know that without wasting any more time, they launched their idea. The four friends climbed onto the roof, pitched up ol' Reuben after them, and proceeded to execute "Plan A" with a passion! Now, I have no idea where they mustered up such courage! There must have been such an urgency to the project that they didn't even stop to calculate what the repair bill would be for Peter's roof. (If they had known the reputation of this rough fisherman or his volatile outbursts, I'd rather doubt that they would have carried out this scheme!)

Nevertheless, their plan was followed through with until poor Reuben lay helplessly dangling in front of our Guest Speaker. Above, four pairs of onlooking eyes curiously gazed through the newly crafted "sky light." The room went into an uncomfortable silence as everyone held their breath awaiting the response, or reprimand of the Master.

What would the scribes think? What would the Law demand? Would the Teacher chide the zealous, unthinking friends? Would He demand them to be responsible for immediate repairs?

Jesus' response holds for us a leadership principle that is worth a pound of gold. Instead of chastising them for their ill-planned exploit, He looked straight at the four zealous entrepreneurs and the Bible records these words:

"And Jesus **seeing their faith** said to the paralytic, 'My son, your sins are forgiven'" (Mark 2:5 emphasis added).

He could have chided them for their lack of preplanning. He could have pointed out their tardiness due to their own procrastination and late departure. But instead, He saw their faith! He saw the actions and attempts of Reuben's friends and called it "faith"!

A Leader Sees What's Best

Look for the faith of those around you. Look for evidences of God's presence, not evidences of His absence. In each of us is a measure of faith, a desire for God's best. In every person is a yearning to do well and to make a difference. God created us that way! Those dreams may yet be inside each one of us, and they're somewhat fragile. There will always be novice attempts to fly those dreams.

Sometimes in an attempt to get the plane off the tarmac, those attempts may resemble the dance of a disoriented albatross more than the take-off of an F-22 fighter jet. But encourage them. See the faith and the heart that they're putting behind what they're attempting to do. While the execution of those dreams may still require further development, the potential that remains inside each of us is a precious commodity to God! See people through the eyes of Jesus, and you watch! I'll guarantee that you'll begin to see more miracles on the increase and justifications for why they are not happening on the decrease!

Some of the greatest discoveries came from people readjusting their eyes to see what's best about a situation rather than what's worse. I heard a story about George De Mestral who was out walking his dog one afternoon. The dog got loose for a moment and ran through some tall grass. When he finally retrieved his wayward pet, the dog was covered with burrs tangled in his fur. When he arrived home, George could have cursed the dog while cutting the burrs out. Instead, he decided to take a cutting of the fur and view it under his microscope. Amazed at it gripping characteristics, he decided to study it even further. It was his curiosity and his willingness to see its potential that ultimately led to him to the creating of Velcro!

How to Please God

Now let me make a disclaimer here. As wonderful as it is to have leaders who believe in us, in the final analysis, it will be our own responsibility to develop our gifts. No one else's. *We* will be held accountable for whether we've invested them or buried them. Matthew 25 holds a clear teaching on investing what God has entrusted to us.

> "And the one also who had received the one talent came up and said, ... 'I was afraid, and went away and hid your talent in the ground; see, you have what is yours.' But his master answered and said to him, 'You wicked, lazy slave, you knew that I reap where I did not sow, and gather where I scattered no seed. Then you ought to have put my money in the bank, and on my arrival I would have received my money back with interest. Therefore take away the talent from him, and give it to the one who has the ten talents. For to everyone who has shall more be given, and he shall have an abundance; but from the one who does not have, even what he does have shall be taken away'" (Matthew 25:24-29).

There are many applications to this story, but one message rings true: "You can't please God by not investing what you have!" In order to please God, we must use our gifts. It would be better to have risked for God and come up short than to have never attempted at all.

You Develop Gifts by Risking for God

Leaders develop their gifts by "going for it." There are no shortcuts. If it's for God, don't ask "Why?" Ask "Why not?" Matthew tells us that we can't please God if we play it safe. God is pleased when we are willing to risk what we have for the sake of the Master. Too many of us are afraid, so we bury our gifts, and we wonder why we never grow or increase in our giftedness and influence. In fact, one of the keys to the success of the early Church is found in Acts 15:25-26 where "Barnabas and Paul ... men who have risked their lives for the name of our Lord Jesus Christ."

One of my favorite verses is found in Proverbs 14:4. "Where no oxen are, the manger is clean, but much increase comes by the strength of the ox." In other words, strength will always bring with it problems, but that's normal! Don't be afraid of mistakes. Be willing to risk for God! If your goal is to keep a clean manger, than you won't need any oxen, but if your desire is to make a difference with your life, then you'll need to be ready to clean up some doo doo's. You see, if you're afraid of messes, if you're afraid of failing, if you're afraid of risking, you'll never get anywhere. As one man said, "You can't steal second base with your foot still on first." You've got to be willing to go for it!

In Hawaii, I often hear advertisements beckoning potential travelers to Las Vegas for a weekend of gambling. The fares are very reasonable and the hotel rooms are at bargain prices. Of course the plan is to lure you so that you'll spend your hard-earned dollars on the roulette tables or watch them disappear into one of the many one-armed bandits that line the casinos. Each year, thousands of residents flock to these hollow Promised Lands to risk their savings in hopes of striking it rich. We think nothing of taking risks with our money, even though, knowing that there is more chance of returning home empty handed than there is returning a millionaire.

C.T. Studd, a great preacher of yesteryear once said, "The gamblers for gold are so many, but the gamblers for God are so few. Where are the gamblers for God!"

We risk our lives each time we fly in an airplane. We take a risk when we invest in a stock. We take a risk when we get married. We take a risk when we buy a house. I think it's high time we risk for God! He's so much worthier than any earthly investment we can find!

I remember a great little poem that reminds us that life is made up of many risks.

"There once lived a man who never risked, he never tried. He never laughed, he never prayed, he never cried. Then one day when he passed away, his insurance was denied. They said since he never really lived, then he never really died!"—Anonymous

You will develop your gifts by using them. Sure it may include some risks. The risk of making a mistake, the risk of faltering or stammering if you speak. But go for it! Don't wait until your gifts they are fully developed before you put them into use. That won't happen because gifts don't ripen like a bunch of bananas put in a dark place. Gifts treated in the same way don't ripen. They get rotten!

Your gifts develop and ripen by using them!

Take Me Out to the Ballgame!

As an example, let's say that during a revival campaign, you received the gift of, well, er..., professional baseball! (Just for the sake of dialogue, mind you.) Hands were laid on your head and this wonderful gift was bestowed on you. But even though this gift is now in you, you still look the same, act the same, and walk the same. What do you have to do to see this gift come to pass? What must you do in order for it to blossom and mature?

You have to play baseball!

So you get out on the field. You've never swung a bat before. The coach steps up to the pitcher's mound and you to the plate. The coach pitches the first ball, you swing and miss it by a mile. Do you quit now? No! You dust yourself off and take another pitch. The coach encourages you.

"It's in you! Swing again. I know it's in you!"

So you take your stance in the batter's box, and the second pitch comes whizzing by and smacks into the catcher's glove. You didn't even see it go by!

"It's in you. Swing the bat next time. Swing the bat!" the coach encourages you.

The third pitch is hurled. You close your eyes and swing with all your might.

KABOOM!

The ball rockets off the sweet spot of the ol' Louisville Slugger and sails into the outfield!

"That's it!" shouts the coach. "I knew you had it in you. Keep it up, now. Keep it up!"

As the months go by, you continue training. The balls are going further and further. Out in the field at shortstop, nothing gets by you. Double plays, then triple plays! You begin to love this sport! Every chance you get, you can be found on the baseball diamond, fielding grounders or hitting home runs.

Now fast-forward the tape about three years. An exhibition game is being held between two championship teams, one of which is yours. Your reputation as a promising rookie spreads, and a couple of scouts from the Atlanta Braves fly in for the game.

They watch you hit, field, and run the bases like a pro. In the fourth inning, just after one of your spectacular double plays, one scout leans over to the other and remarks, "You see that kid? Now, he has a gift. That kid has a gift!"

And they're right, but how did that gift get developed? How did it come to its fullness?

You had to play baseball!

This principle applies to doing church as a team. Use your gift! Even though you miss a few grounders, stay in there. It's in you! When you strike out, swing again. It's in you! I know it!

Say "yes" more often than you say "no." Get involved. If after awhile, you find your piece of the puzzle just doesn't fit, simply move laterally to something else, but keep serving! Pretty soon you'll be knocking the ball out of the park, and people will look at you and exclaim, "Wow. You are so gifted! How did that happen?"

And you'll reply, "Just play baseball."

Building Your Character Before Building Your Ministry

I was a new Christian, I taught several morning Bible studies. We would often meet at restaurants and along with a group of seven or eight men, we would pour over the Scriptures along with numerous cups of coffee for an hour or so before going to work. Looking back on those years, I recall that I learned more from teaching than I ever gave out. I often think that God had me teach those studies not so much for what would happen *through* me as much as what would happen *in* me. You see, God is less interested in what you are *doing* and much more interested in what you're *becoming*.

As I look back over the years, I have seen many times where my involvement had little to do with what I could contribute and a whole lot more to do with God building my character through what I was doing! Sometimes the Lord will place you in a position for a certain season because He knows that there are some things that need to be developed in you. When you get involved, God will be instilling character or virtue in you through the process. It may be the quality of endurance, submission, people skills, or building positive attitudes.

Following is a letter taken from a book I wrote to my children called *Gems Along The Way*:

Dear Amy, Aaron, and Abby,

I saw a lady's four-carat diamond ring the other day. Wow! Was that ever impressive! The diamond must have been worth $20,000! (I'm not a diamond appraiser or anything, but after considering it for a moment, I felt strongly that such a diamond would surely detract from the natural beauty of your mother's hand, so I didn't buy it.)

Anyway, the gold band was a simple one with a few smaller diamonds on either side. Holding the diamond in place was a setting that included maybe five or six prongs.

"My!" I thought. "That setting had better be strong! It's holding onto $20,000!"

Although the setting doesn't get as much attention as the diamond itself, it is equally as important. Any wise jeweler would never put such a precious jewel in a poor or weak setting! If he did, then one small bump and the gem would be lost! The strength and quality of the setting will determine the security and staying power of the gem!

Character is like that setting. God has promised us such wonderful gems! Yet, without the basis of character, His promises would be lost or forfeited at the first bump! The Holy Spirit's desire is to produce character in each of us prior to the setting of the gems. Whether those gems are marriage, an influential position, a ministry, finances, or a family, each of these will require character. This is the setting that needs to be developed prior to the placement of the gem.

Strengthen your setting. Build your character. Learn to forgive, to be diligent, to be honest. Learn to stay steady and faithful, to keep commitments, to go by what you know and not necessarily by what you feel.

Here's a simple definition of character that I heard along the way:

Character is the ability to follow through on a worthy decision long after the emotion of making that decision has passed.

God will refine your metal till it's pure gold. He will shape your character till it's strong and trustworthy. Then when God sees that the setting is ready, He will be faithful to place His very best gems in your life! That's when you'll shine!

Love, Dad

Over the long haul, ministry should charge you up. You'll build character along the way, but if coming away from your ministry week after week finds you drained, stop! Reevaluate what may be causing this and find a remedy. Don't keep running on empty! Sometimes it may be God working on your character, and sometimes it may be time for you to move. Either is fine. Just be sure that if you move, you are always following the leading of the Lord, and not running from a problem.

In the past, I have experienced overwhelming feelings that had nothing to do with my placement. It had more to do with my character development than it did with gifts or passion. What we often see defined as "burn-out" can be personality conflicts or problems with submission to authority. These are character issues that God wants to deal with once and for all! If we bail out, the lesson will only have to be repeated in another setting. Second verse, same as the first.

This is where accountability through friendships has become a lifesaver for me. I need people watching out for me, and I need to do the same for others. Develop deep enough relationships along the way that you are willing to allow others to speak into your life. Being committed to one another's success is an irreducible in doing church as a team. If we could do that for each other ... (you may sing this next line) "What a wonderful world this would be!"

Security Check-Point

Developing servant-leaders will always require one major ingredient: security. Without being secure as a leader, you will find it virtually impossible to attract, develop, or retain other leaders. You cannot do church as a team while battling insecurity. Good leaders are able to build confidence in others.

Secure people encourage others and they enjoy the successes of others. They can applaud other's achievements and they love making them successful. These leaders are constantly appreciating the efforts of others. Secure leaders are neither territorial nor possessive. They are able to surround themselves with people more qualified than themselves.

Insecure people feel that if they are not controlling everything around them, then they're not doing their job. They fear criticism and worry about what others think. When that happens, they can never believe that others are competent enough to do the job. Hence, they seldom delegate anything at all! Leaders must always remember that everyone will make mistakes, and often, those are the best classrooms in the world!

Take a look at yourself as a leader. You will do well and score high points if you will "catch people doing things right," and by showing a genuine excitement for their accomplishments! It is well said that we'd be surprised how much can be accomplished if we don't care who gets the credit!

Take a look at this Ten Point checklist and see how you fare:

A SECURE LEADER:	AN INSECURE LEADER:
Encourages other's attempts	Sabotages other's efforts
Points out other's strong points	Brings attention to other's faults
Overlooks flaws	Uses other's flaws as ammunition
Readily admits own mistakes	Is defensive and justifies mistakes
Gives away credit to others	Demands or manipulates credit
Rejoices when others succeed	Gets jealous with other's successes
Gets excited when others do it better	Gets easily intimidated
Willing to risk to improve	Plays it safe to retain position
Is content to remain anonymous	Requires others to notice
Is quick to build teams	Wants to do things himself

What kind of leader are you? How did you score? Are you someone who can "catch people doing something right?" Can you easily give credit away and genuinely show an excitement for the accomplishments of others? How hard is it for you to build teams? Let's take a look at how that can be done.

Passing Out Batons and Running Together

I noticed something interesting about the leadership style of Jesus. He began passing batons to His disciples early in His ministry. In the sixth chapter of Mark, He is already choosing twelve to succeed Him. Passing batons isn't to be a last-ditch effort. Plan on it. Start it early on in your ministry.

I enjoyed studying the missionary efforts of old Hawaii. Titus Coan became one of my heroes, as did Hiram Bingham. They served the people of Hawaii during the early and mid 1800's. They did hundreds of things right. But I noticed two things that hindered the future of their ministries.

The first was that they lost their second generation. Their children grew up without a deep and genuine faith. There may have been many reasons for that, but suffice it to say that their plates were probably so full that they had little time left for their own children. That is a poignant lesson for all of us!

The second thing I caught was that they passed the baton too late in life. Just before expiring, Titus Coan passed the mantle of leadership to a few potential leaders. They carried on as best they could, but inevitably, the mission diminished and the vision faded. It may take only a moment to pass a baton, but it takes much longer to pass the heart of that baton. In doing church as a team, passing out batons early insures that no one burns out and that we all share the joys (and sorrows) together! In New Hope, we don't pass batons as a precursor that marks the end of one's ministry. We pass out batons as a way of including others in on the race!

You don't pass the baton in a relay race when you are pooped out! You pass it at the very apex of your stride. The same is true in doing church as a team. Invite others into your ministry! Pass batons. Include new people, and don't be intimidated when others do it better! God will always have a place for you, and the greater a servant you are, the greater the joy you'll experience. Your gift may be to build platforms for other emerging leaders. When they are successful, you build more!

One of the fastest and easiest ways to pass batons is through shadowing. We recommend this in almost every volunteer ministry in New Hope. It is a way of introducing others to your ministry. Shadowing is simply following someone around who has been serving in an area of interest to you. It's a low-risk orientation that gives you a glimpse of what is being done. It's also an opportunity to build new friendships along the way!

The three stages of shadowing are:

Stage 1—I do, you watch.

Stage 2—We do together.

Stage 3—You do, I applaud!

That's the heart behind passing batons.

When Amy, my daughter, was a senior, she ran for the relay team of her high school. I noticed they practiced one thing again and again. They would all line up facing the same direction, about an arm's length apart from each other. While running in place, they would practice passing the baton from one runner to the other. When it was passed from the front to the back, they'd repeat the process till the timing and the passes were perfected. The reason? In a relay, the race will be either won or lost in the passing of the baton.

Include Others Early On

Passing the baton is actually our willingness to allow God to use us in building and including others. It is our openness to being used by the Holy Spirit in helping others to become successful! This is all part of what it means to do church as a team. I guess instead of talking about "passing the baton," it would better be described as "passing out batons." Unlike a relay team, you pass batons to all of the team members. Then you run together! You don't pass a baton then quit. You stay with the team, and you run together!

Passing the baton is our willingness to build and include others.

When we look at the larger picture of God's plan for the church in the community, we can easily see that passing batons is crucial. Lateral moves will be something common, but building teams that run together is even more important! Learn to pass out batons. Do it early. Don't wait until the end. Invite others into your ministry and readily applaud their successes. Fight the tendency to become territorial or possessive. That will only bring havoc to new and emerging leaders. An open welcome is important in developing an atmosphere of growth and involvement.

Passing out batons allows for each of us to begin by first serving one another. Have you ever wondered why Jesus sent out His disciples two-by-two? May I suggest that it was because He knew that the credibility of the Gospel would best be seen in the context of relationships. As people witnessed the love and friendship, the care and camaraderie of the two messengers, they would give credence to the message!

Start by Serving Each Other

Although we realize that serving the Lord and others are best done in teams, we know that one of the things that makes this happen is by first serving the others on your team! Some call this "lateral serving." Here, serving one another is given equal importance as serving to get something accomplished. This is the "esprit de corps" of the church.

Lateral serving is the opposite of saying "it's not my ministry or responsibility." It's instead a willingness to occasionally do someone else's job with great joy. It is seeing a task that has been overlooked by another and gratefully filling in. Someone said that it is the "art of making good on someone else's mistake." We see the importance of "cross training" so we can better serve others when they need a break or if they simply need our support. There will be times when each of our flames will dwindle, and that's when we need each other the most.

One man said that you never diminish the flame of your own candle by lighting the flame of someone else.

I like that. ✗

CHAPTER SIX STUDY GUIDE

"Developing Servant-Leaders"

1. What are the greatest fears that people have about getting involved in ministry? List three of them:

   a.

   b.

   c.

2. What remedies would you give that would dispel each of these fears?

   a.

   b.

   c.

3. Often we find that God is less interested in what you are doing and more interested with what you are becoming! Make a list of some character qualities you have learned along the way. Can you remember specific instances?

4. List and discuss some of the fears people have in allowing others to be included in ministry?

Setting Your Compass

Chapter Seven

Setting Your Compass

"If you don't know where you're going, any road will get you there."

—◆——◆—

It was in the classic "Alice in Wonderland" that Alice encounters the Red Queen in a hurried attempt to find her way through the maze of this fairy tale forest. "Which way do I go?" Alice cried. "Well, that all depends on where you want to go," the Red Queen answered almost nonchalantly. "Well, to tell you the truth," Alice continued, "I really don't know!" The Red Queen concluded, "Then it really doesn't matter which direction you take, does it?"

Before you build a house, you need a blueprint. Before a plane leaves the tarmac, the pilot must file his flight plan with the tower. Before you do church as a team, there must be a clear and concise understanding of the mission and assignment the Lord has given to that specific local church. Each church will have its own community, its own purpose, culture, passion and gifts. God has a very special vision tailor made for your church just as He has one tailor made for you! This vision will become the very foundation of your ministry, the direction for your planning, and the reason for your existence! By keeping this vision clearly fixed. You'll have a much better chance of fulfilling His purposes.

—◆

In this chapter, we will discuss one of the most important aspects of "Doing Church as a Team:" Setting Your Compass.

Then the Lord answered me and said, "Record the vision and inscribe it on tablets, that the one who reads it may run" (Hab. 2:2).

What is a Vision?

A sculptor named Gutzon Borglum is credited for the magnificent carving of Abraham Lincoln at the Capitol in Washington, D.C. He chipped it from one large stone in his studio. The story is told of the cleaning lady that swept up for him every day. Many months passed, and the moment of the unveiling finally arrived. Gutzon Borglum invited this faithful cleaning lady to the inaugural showing as his invited guest. When the velvet drape was removed, the room was filled with the sounds of awe struck admirers. The beauty of this work of art was stunning. Smooth lines, the clear features of Lincoln's face, the jutting jaw, and pronounced cheekbones all expressed the touch of a master sculptor.

The evening came to a close with the artist and the cleaning woman staring at the finished piece of artwork that would adorn the capitol for generations to come. "Well, what do you think?" the sculptor asked. After a brief moment, this faithful worker calmly replied, "I have only one question. How did you know that Mr. Lincoln was in that rock?"

Vision is the ability to see what others may not. It is the capacity to see potential, what things *could* be. It is the ability to see what God sees, and the God given motivation to bring what you see to pass! Whether it is a personal vision or a vision for the church, this is what stirs up your faith! You can't have one without the other. Faith will birth vision, and a vision will fuel your faith. Hebrews 11:1 describes that kind of vision: "Now faith is the substance of things hoped for, the evidence of things unseen." We need faith to see the unseen, and by seeing what God sees for your future, you begin to have vision. This is how you begin to see, not only with your eyes but also with your heart.

Steven Covey in his book, *Seven Habits of Highly Effective People* talks about "beginning with the end in mind." He based this on the principle that everything has been created twice: once in the mind of imagination where only you can see it, and then it comes to pass in the physical realm where it becomes tangible and everyone else can see it. When you can conceive a clear picture of what God's blueprint is for your life or that of the church, you begin to have vision! The clearer the picture, the better your chances are of others catching it and buying into it. Especially as a pastor, this step is absolutely critical. There are no shortcuts on this one.

What can you believe God for? Much of your future will be based on this one question. "As Jesus left the house, he was followed by two blind men crying out, 'Mercy, Son of David! Mercy on us!' When Jesus got home, the blind men went in with him. Jesus said to them, 'Do you really believe that I can do this?' They said, 'Why, yes, Master!' *He* touched their eyes and said, **'Become what you believe.'** It happened. They saw" (Matthew 9:27-30 The Message Bible, emphasis mine). We become what we believe. If you can't believe that God will do something wonderful, you'll have what you believe.

I play the guitar. Not well, mind you, but I love the sound of the guitar. I have for years. One day when I was living in Eugene, Oregon, I was invited by my guitar teacher to listen to a great jazz guitarist produce the most beautiful melodic lines I had ever heard. I was in awe of how his skilled fingers moved with such ease and clarity. I turned to my teacher and said, "Man, I could never play like that!"

He turned and with a slow reply as if to add emphasis to his words, "That's why you don't. You can't believe that you could do it. And you won't until you can change your mind!"

One man says, "I can," and another says, "I can't." Which one is correct?

Both.

"As a man thinks, so is he" (Prov.23:7).

It's Never Too Late to Start Dreaming

The first step in finding your vision is to dream. That's right! God loves dreamers. It is dreamers who bring about the changes our world so desperately needs. It is the dreamers that God uses to turn dying churches into vibrant communities of excited people. Joseph was a dreamer, and God used him to deliver a whole nation out of bondage! God taught Abraham how to dream. In Genesis 15:5, God took Abraham outside of his tent and said, "Now look toward the heavens, and count the stars, if you are able to count them." And He said to him, "So shall your descendants be." When Abraham caught it, God commended him and "reckoned it to him as righteousness." God wanted Abraham to have a clear picture of the end result of His promise.

In Joel 2:28, God lets us in on one aspect of the Holy Spirit's ministry toward us in these last days. "And it will come about after this that I will pour out My Spirit on all mankind; and your sons and daughters will prophesy, your old men will dream dreams, your young men will see visions." Zero in with me on the phrase, "your old men will dream dreams." There can be several applications for this phrase, but let me suggest just one that I think applies to each and every one of us: It's never too late to start dreaming again! That's right. Many have stopped dreaming, and with it comes the end of visionaries. Nothing happens until someone starts to dream! Some of you reading this might think that it's too late; that you'll never amount to anything. I have good news for you! That is one of the very reasons the Holy Spirit is being poured out on us as Christians in these last days! Why? So we can dream again!

Remember that nothing happens in a church until someone starts to dream. A church will never outgrow its vision, and no vision will ever exceed its leaders' ability to dream. So dream big dreams for God! One of the reasons many of us lose motivation is that we've stopped dreaming about what wonderful things God can do for our futures, our churches, our families, and our finances.

"Dream lofty dreams, and as you dream, so shall you become. Your vision is the promise of what you shall one day be!"—James Allen

When Disneyworld in Orlando opened some years ago, the widow of the great entrepreneur stood with one of the engineers of this expansive entertainment center gazing at its magnificence and beauty. The engineer in a genuine effort to honor one of our country's greatest innovators, turned toward Mrs. Disney and remarked, "Boy, I wish Walt could have seen this!" Without taking her eyes off the sprawling view of this beautiful playland, she confidently replied, "He did. That's why it's here."

God wants us to start dreaming again. That's the beginning of God-glorifying vision. Dream up the best thing you can for your life. If you are a pastor, dream up the best vision you can for the church. Fast-forward the tape ten years down the road. If there were no restrictions whatsoever, what could you see? Make the dream as lofty as you can. Even if it seems outrageous, fix it in your mind. Got it? Now read this verse from Ephesians 3:20 in the Living Bible:

"Now glory be to God, who by his mighty power at work within us is able to do far more than we would ever dare to ask or even dream of—infinitely beyond our highest prayers, desires, thoughts, or hopes."

Do you see what He is saying? Go ahead. Dream the biggest dreams you can because when you do, God's dreams for you will always be bigger still!

Blowing a Clear Trumpet

"The Lord spoke further to Moses, saying, 'Make yourself two trumpets of silver, of hammered work you shall make them; and you shall use them for summoning the congregation and for having the camps set out'" (Nu. 10:1-2).

Once God gives you a God-glorifying dream of what your ministry can be, the next step is to hammer it out. This step is probably the most time consuming but also the most important. Take the time necessary to plot your course carefully in the beginning so you won't be having to make major course corrections in the future. The time you spend on this point will save you many sorrows in the years to come. Especially if you are a new pastor of a church, based on your gifts and leadership style, a couple of silver trumpets will need to be hammered out. You may use the same materials, same purpose and same assignment as before, but hammer it out again till it blows clearly for you!

In this portion of Scripture, God spoke to Moses about his assignment. He commanded Moses to "Make for yourself two trumpets of silver, of hammered work shall you make them." Now I want you to notice that God commanded Moses to "make for yourself" these trumpets. He was not to buy them, rent them, or use someone else's! He was to hammer it out for himself and then learn to blow it until it would sound clearly! These were to be used to call the congregation together, to summon leaders, warn the people, and to give organization to their travel plans when God told them to move.

> "And when both are blown, all the congregation shall gather themselves to you at the doorway of the tent of meeting. Yet if only one is blown, then the leaders, the heads of the divisions of Israel, shall assemble before you. But when you blow an alarm, the camps that are pitched on the east side shall set out." (Nu. 10:3-5).

I noticed something else that was interesting in the early stages of Israel's vision building. God told Moses to make for himself "two trumpets." God had in mind from the very beginning that Moses was to work in teams. God designed it in such a way that he was to recruit and train others from the very beginning! You see, Moses only had one set of lips, but God required two trumpets to be blown! Someone had to be shadowing Moses and learning how to lead as a team!

Begin With What You Have

Usually at the beginning stages, we will have the tendency to feel inadequate for the tasks ahead. We will feel ill equipped to measure up to any new vision, let alone a God-glorifying dream! I'm sure Moses felt this way too. So did David, Peter, the Apostle Paul, and so will we. But here's some good news. Start with what you have! God doesn't need much! A few loaves and a couple of dried fish will do!

When God ordered Moses to convince Pharaoh that God had sent him, Moses would have loved to use eloquent speech, but he didn't possess eloquent speech. He could have used prominence or a position of authority to assist with his persuasion, but he didn't have either. All he had was a staff in his hand, but that's all God needed to start with! He ordered Moses to throw it down, and it became a serpent. With that, God began His miracles!

David Livingstone was one of Christianity's greatest missionaries to Africa. He not only brought the Gospel to the natives of this vast country, but he lived it as well. This gave him great favor in the hearts of the people of Africa. David felt God asking him to penetrate further into the Congo to bring the message of Jesus Christ to those who had never heard it before. Upon arriving at one of the tribes in the interior, the custom was to first call for an audience with the tribal chief before entering. To not comply with this could cost him his life.

This entrance test would require David to wait outside the gate of this tribe with all his possessions lined up next to him. The chief, as a sign of acceptance and entry, would take whatever his heart so desired from among the missionary's possessions, and to complete the exchange, would give David one of his own. Then and only then, would he be authorized to enter and share his message of the Gospel. So there he was. The scene resembled an orderly garage sale complete with his Bible, writing pad, clothes, shoes, blanket, and at the end of the line, his goat. You see, David Livingstone's weak stomach required that he drink goat's milk on a daily basis for his ailment. The drinking water was often questionable, so this was the safest answer to his survival. Often he had prayed asking God to heal this infirmity, but until that time, he seemed sentenced to drinking goat's milk every morning.

After what seemed an eternity of waiting, the chief emerged from his tent and made his way slowly towards this man of God he had heard so much about. Ornately decked with ivory and gold, he walked towards the gate being followed closely by his advisors and priests. The chief surveyed the possessions of this great missionary. Secretly, David prayed, "Lord, let him take anything he wants except my goat! You know that I need its milk for my very survival! Lord, blind his eyes to the goat!"

Whether it was that God heard and chose not to answer, or that He had other plans, it was not revealed to David. The chief promptly walked over to the goat, pointed at it, and within moments, one of his advisors has whisked the animal away! David stood stunned! It seemed as if his life had abruptly come to a halt.

In a few moments, the one that took his goat to an adjacent pen returned. In exchange, he handed David a stick, and left.

"A stick!" David cried. "This is ridiculous! Here he takes my life's sustenance, and in return, I get this old stick!"

A man standing close by, noticing the confusion quickly spoke.

"Oh no. That is not a stick. My friend, that is the chief's very own scepter. With it, you will gain entry to every tribe and village in the interior. You have been given safe passage and great authority as a gift from the king!"

It was then that David realized what God had done. From that point on, God's Word spread to thousands and thousands of people, and on a side note, God healed David Livingstone's stomach as well!

God will always start with what you have, not with what you do not have. God said to make the trumpets of silver, but where in the world would they get silver? No jewelry stores were to be found in the desert neighborhood, I'm sure. So where would this precious commodity be found? It was mined from the people themselves. They had plundered the Egyptians prior to exiting their bondage of slavery and had collected articles of gold and silver (Ex. 12:35-36). All that was required was found within their grasp! The trumpets were made out of what they had, not out of what they didn't.

All you need is within your grasp. Don't fret over what you don't have. Start with what you do! Don't worry about perfection. God will tune up your vision along the way, but start with a God-glorifying dream. Write it down and hammer it out. Then keep hammering until it blows clearly!

Custom Trumpets Only, Please!

There will be trumpets for sale everywhere, trumpets that have been forged and hammered out by others. They'll be for sale and readily available in every city, at most conferences, through the magazines and through mail order, but don't buy them! You can buy trumpets from Chicago, Los Angeles, Korea, Toronto, Brownsville, or even Hawaii. But don't do it. Hammer it out for yourself! Sure it will take some time and effort, but it's worth it! Then and only then will it blow clearly!

What are the things we should take back from these ministries?

Take back "hammering techniques." Learn principles and new perspectives, but don't buy ready-made trumpets. The reason they work so well in their own specific communities is that they have taken the time to hammer it out for themselves. Each of us must do the same! And when you take the time to hammer it out, you will find a depth of understanding and a quality that could never have been attained any other way. You'll begin to blow a clarion sound that will help others to catch the vision and do church as a team!

"The harder the conflict, the more glorious the triumph. What we obtain too cheaply, we esteem too lightly; 'tis dearness only that gives everything its value." — Thomas Paine

Guidelines for a God-Glorifying Vision

Every church needs a clear vision with these qualities:

The Vision Must Be Birthed and Aligned with the Word Of God

(2 Tim. 3:16,17) It is God's Word that is infallible, not my desires or goals. Be sure that the Bible confirms your dreams, never conflicting with it. Is there a key scripture that embodies your vision? Ask God to reveal it to you. He will.

The Vision Must Be Hammered Out

(Nu. 10:1-2) It must be clear and concise, easily understood by everyone (Hab. 2:2). Your whole heart must be in the vision. If it is not, if it is simply another program from another ministry, you will not pursue it aggressively. If God has indeed given you a vision, then He will give you the passion to fuel that vision and see it come to pass. He will also make available all the resources needed to see it through!

The Vision Must Be Consistent With the Great Commission in Reaching the Lost

(Mt. 28:19-20) Every church should have at its core a passion for the lost. We can have goals for success, nurturing, and discipleship, but if people are not ultimately coming to Christ, we have missed the point!

The Vision Must Guide Every Activity

(John 13:17) It cannot be a neat platitude or a nice saying in a booklet somewhere. It must become the compass that guides all our activities. Churches without a clear commission or statement of purpose are like ships without rudders. Make it plain and always visible as a reminder of God's call for the church.

Each of us is accountable to run the race that God has set before us. The writer of Hebrews admonishes us to "run with endurance the race that is set before us..." (Heb. 12:1). The same is true for congregations. Every church has a specific race, a unique assignment, and an assigned direction. We will stand accountable for the completion and fulfillment of that call. Not all churches are the same. Each has its own unique style or thumbprint, and that assignment must be processed and refined until everyone feels an ownership in it.

How New Hope Did It

"Go therefore and make disciples of all the nations, baptizing them in the name of the Father and the Son and the Holy Spirit, teaching them to observe all that I commanded you; and lo, I am with you always, even to the end of the age" (Mt. 28:19-20).

Here we find the "Great Commission" that Jesus left to us. From this one verse, we find the starting point for all assignments. This is the heart of Jesus for the church as well as for the lost, and it is here that we in New Hope found our call and assignment.

The Great Commission can easily be broken into four distinct stages.

Stage One

The first word tells us to "GO!" This means action! Jesus calls us to take the initiative and reach out! We call this EVANGELISM. This is simply taking non-Christians and leading them to the Lord in such a way that they become Christians: transformed, forgiven, and growing followers of Christ! But God never told the world to come to the Church. He told the Church to "go into all the world!" Therefore, we must each take the initiative to reach out to our families and friends, inviting them to Jesus!

Our Sunday morning services are designed to partner with our members in their attempts to win their friends and families to Christ. The ambiance, printed materials, music and message are all shaped to support this one goal.

Stage Two

The second stage we find here is discipleship: "...make disciples of all nations, baptizing them in the name of the Father, and the Son, and the Holy Spirit." We call this EDIFICATION, or building each individual up in their faith. God never said to fill the churches with "converts." He said to fill them with "disciples." Our goal is to take a convert and build him or her into a disciple of the Lord. This is where our small groups and midweek services come in. New Hope has a course and tape series called *Growing Deep, Growing Strong* that introduces each person to membership.

Stage Three

The third stage alludes to a further EQUIPPING where God encourages each of us "to observe all I have commanded you." This is putting into practice what we understand. Herein lies the beginning of fruitfulness and life transformation. It is not just in the knowing, but in the doing that we are blessed. Jesus tells us this in John: "If you know these things, you are blessed if you do them" (John 13:17 emphasis added).

The New Hope DESIGN course plays a large part on this stage. Equipping people by helping them discover, develop, and deploy their gifts helps them to grow. It is here that each person is encouraged to put his or her gifts into action.

Stage Four

Then finally, Jesus calls us to take courage in reaching out to others. The Lord assures us that He will accompany us: "And lo, I am with you even until the end of the age." We call this EXTENSION. This closes the "loop" with each of us now reaching out and inviting someone else, even as we were invited!

From this was birthed the Mission Statement of New Hope Christian Fellowship:

The Purpose of New Hope is to present the Gospel of Jesus Christ in such a way that turns non-Christians into converts (Evangelism), converts into disciples (Edification), and disciples into mature, fruitful leaders (Equipping), who will in turn go into the world and reach others for Christ (Extension).

This overarching purpose guides everything we do. This is the "trumpet" of New Hope that we use to summon people towards God's purposes. It must be blown consistently and clearly in order for us to paddle together as a team, each of us heading toward the same common direction with the same heart and same goals. In the next chapter, we will discuss how to get everyone pulling in the same direction.

"For if the bugle produces an indistinct sound, who will prepare himself for battle?" (I Cor. 14:8).

Aligning Your Vision

There's one thing worse than a church without vision. It's a church with many visions! In this kind of congregation, everyone is lobbying for their own personal agendas and the church ends up becoming a political body of individuals, each one pulling for his or her own viewpoint. With too many visions, a church will have the seeds of dissension at its very inception. An old Greek proverb says, "If you pursue two hares, both will escape you."

" ... make my joy complete by being of the same mind, maintaining the same love, united in spirit, intent on one purpose" (Phil. 2:2).

Here, Paul speaks about the joy of everyone possessing the same heart and passion. This is something called alignment. Alignment is simply everyone pulling in the same direction. It's having all the arrows pointing the same way! This is one of the most powerful concepts in building teams.

There's nothing more beautiful than a church where everyone has the same starting point, the same heart, the same direction, and the same cadence. This is what gives the rhythm and brings harmony! Without this, disharmony and disunity will prevail. When individuals lobby for their own ideas, conflict is sure to erupt. On the other hand, alignment can build an unstoppable movement that can overcome every obstacle, move every mountain, and bridge every impasse. With alignment, each daily activity will contribute in a more meaningful way to the overall vision of the church.

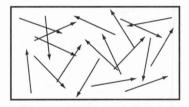 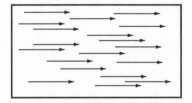

CHURCH WITHOUT ALIGNMENT   CHURCH WITH ALIGNMENT

Just as we have many members in our physical bodies, there will be many ministries in any healthy church: youth, men's, women's, small groups, and children's, to name a few. When there is alignment, each ministry should be constantly evaluating itself. It must continually review how strategic it is in fulfilling the church's overall vision.

Each ministry must ask itself:

- Is our ministry producing disciples and mature leaders who can integrate into the context of the church, or is it an island in itself with independent goals?

- Is our ministry resulting in men and women coming to Christ?

- If yes, then are these new converts being discipled?

- Are they discovering, developing, and deploying their spiritual gifts in such a way that causes others to know Christ?

Building a Common Culture

When each individual ministry and every individual member begins pulling in the same direction, you begin doing church as a team. It builds a common "culture" where everyone is saying the same thing. For example, let's say that a large supermarket hired you. Your job was to stock the shelves, so you arrive at the specified time and you are told to stock the canned goods along with a few other workers. After a moment or two, you strike up a conversation: "How long you been working here?" "About a year," the other replies. "I just hired on yesterday. I've never met the owner. What kind of place is this to work in?" The other worker gruffly replies, "Just do your job and you won't have any problems. Keep you nose clean, your mouth shut, and your eyes open. Pick up your paycheck and stay out of people's way. Got it?" "I got it!" you reply, and your first day begins. You now have an impression of the whole company even before you meet the owner or the manager. It was the workers that established the culture or atmosphere for you.

Let's say on the other hand, things went a bit differently. You strike up the conversation, "How long you been working here?" "About a year," the other replies. "I just hired on yesterday. I've never met the owner. What kind of place is this to work in?" A second worker turns to you and says, "It's a wonderful place. I mean, it's become like family to me. The owner is caring and interested in everyone. You'll absolutely love it here. It won't be long before you will feel like family too! Here, take a moment and let me introduce you to the other stock clerks!" And off you go with a whole new feeling! Although you've never met the owner, you love the place! You have a deep feeling that you're going to enjoy working here!

You see, everyone has a ministry of "enculturating" new people, and this can only happen when everyone is in agreement with certain core values. When these values are understood and echoed in the heart of every member, you have *alignment*.

What is a Value?

A value can be likened to a "homing device," an internal guidance mechanism that keeps you on course. A value is what helps you to make in-flight corrections to your attitudes, motives, activities, and emphases. You will need to make many in-flight corrections along the way, but if you have not clearly defined your core values, you won't know what to correct to!

Some years ago, I took a week of golf lessons. My instructor's goal was to teach me what the basic swing was to feel like, and how the ball was to fly if I hit it accordingly! The whole week was geared to that one single goal. Without knowledge of the basic swing and what the flight of the ball should look like when I hit it correctly, I would have no point of reference in the future. Without this basic core swing, even should if I have the privilege of hitting a great shot, I wouldn't know what I did to have created such a shot. I wouldn't be able to repeat it even if I tried! Conversely, should I hit a terrible shot, I'd have no idea why it went bad or how to correct it!

A church's core values give each person a point of reference that acts like a gyro, keeping a sense of balance in the ministry. Values are like windows through which decisions are viewed. When we are confronted with a certain choice, we will tend to make a choice consistent to our values. It gives everyone the same starting point, the same perspective, and the same vantage point. When people in the church are making decisions that are consistent with the core values, you achieve a wonderful synergy and culture of balance and health.

In New Hope, our values act like a metronome that keeps all of us paddling with the same cadence. We call these our Core Values. These nine values are actually principles that we all hold tightly to. They flavor every activity and they balance every endeavor. Each member wholeheartedly subscribes to each one. In doing so, we can all "have the same love, united in spirit, and intent on one purpose."

New Hope's Nine Core Values

1.

We believe that every person, Christian and non-Christian alike, is valuable to God and to His Kingdom. Because people are eternally valuable to God, they are to us as well. Responsible evangelism will always be our cause and ongoing discipleship will always be the core of our ministry (Mt. 18:14; Mt. 25:45; 2 Pt. 3:9).

People are precious. They rank very high on God's ledger, and if we are going to be a people after God's own heart, they'd better rank pretty high on ours as well! We must love them with His love and care for them with His compassion. People are eternal, and their eternal welfare is much more important than their present behavior. Looking past "who they are" and seeing them as what "they can be" will always open new doorways to ministry and miracles. This doesn't mean we become "people pleasers." We are here to please an Audience of One! Loving people means that we are committed to God's very best in their lives. If God's best would be to overlook a fault or indiscretion, then we will comply. If God's best is to confront, then with love, we will confront.

Even in the case of evangelism, we must be sensitive to a person's readiness to receive the Gospel. We, as Christians, can be insensitive to people. In our zeal to convert them, we can do more damage than good. We believe that before we evangelize, we must "Emmanuelize." Responsible evangelism and ongoing discipleship are central to our calling.

2.

We believe that "Doing Church as a Team" is God's design for effective ministry. A Spirit-empowered serving with the willing hearted involvement of every person is vital to God's plan being accomplished (Eccl. 4:9-12; Ps.133: 1; Eph. 4:11-16; 1 Pt.2: 4-9).

The day of the Lone Ranger is over. If we are going to be effective into the 21st century, everyone must realize his or her importance to God's plan. We are called the Body of Christ, not the "collection of the body parts of Christ." Everyone has a place, a function, and a purpose, and we must do it as a team! We've got to learn to work together. There's just no substitute for that! And the more people take ownership of the ministry, the stronger the church becomes.

3.

We believe that a simple presentation of Jesus Christ in creative ways will impact and transform lives. Relating to our culture through redeeming the arts while remaining true to the Scriptures is a balance we will always keep. This allows us to present the Gospel in such a way that reaches the heart (1 Cor. 9:22-23; Acts 17:22-34).

People aren't tired of the Gospel. They're tired of the Gospel being presented in tired ways. The Gospel is the power of God to transform lives! It isn't boring! It is powerful. When the Gospel is preached, the Holy Spirit takes down and out drug addicts and turns them into saints! He takes broken marriages and restores them. He takes hopeless lives and breathes new beginnings into them! But remember this one thing. The Holy Spirit's responsibility is to assure that the message is true, not necessarily interesting. That's our responsibility!

So while remaining true to the Scriptures, we think through creative ways to present the claims of Christ. We will use anything we can to help them understand how wonderful and precious the Word of God is. Hebrews tells us that the Word of God is "living and active," so if we can plant it deep in a person's soul, the Lord will do the rest! But first, we must plant it in good soil so it can take root!

I remember when this one fact first struck me. I was reading Matthew 13, the parable of the sower and the seed. Jesus describes the varying soils in which seed is sown, and He likens it to the varying responses of the human heart. In the explanation given by Jesus, He mentions only once where the devil enters the story. And how does the devil find entry? "When anyone hears the word of the kingdom, and **does not understand it**, the evil one comes and snatches away what has been sown in his heart. This is the one on whom seed was sown beside the road" (Mt. 13:19 emphasis mine).

When someone doesn't understand the Word which was sown in his heart, it gives the devil the opportunity to snatch it away! That hit me like a ton of bricks! I thought to myself, "If I am the preacher, and I am sowing the Word, then I must do my best to make sure each listener understands! Now what they do with it after that is up to them, but I must communicate in such a way that the truth impacts their hearts! I've just got to be sure they understand it!"

That one phrase wouldn't leave me alone! For weeks and months I thought about it. The Good News needed to be simple to understand, creative in its presentation, and accurate in its content. I had to take the "cookies off the top shelf and put it on the lower shelves" so everyone could grasp it.

I just had to help people understand the Gospel! If multi-media would help, then I will use it. If a dance, a mime, a song, a sketch will better present the Gospel so people could better understand it, then I will redeem it for the Gospel's sake! If by tap dancing I could help people's eyes see the truths of the Bible, then I will learn to tap dance!

Now we will not use multi-media or the arts just because it's the trend or simply because others are using it. We use the arts because it will help people to better understand the Word! We will never compromise the truths or accuracy of the Bible for an art form. God's Word never changes, but cultures do. Therefore we will anchor ourselves to His ageless truths but gear the style with which we present those truths to the times we are living in.

4.

We believe that every member should commit to a lifestyle of consistent spiritual growth with honest accountability. A genuine love for God is always of first priority. Every Christian should yearn for spiritual growth. Therefore, discipleship through small groups, accountability, and open honesty is critical to maturing in our faith (Mk. 12:29-31; Acts 2:44-47; 1 Pt. 2:2; 1 Tim. 4:7-8; Prov. 27:17).

Our personal spiritual growth is of such importance that it warrants an all-out, no-holds-barred honesty. Our happiness depends on it! You see, there are two kinds of Christians in the world today. One kind knows what to do. The other kind does what he knows! Our ranks are crowded with the first. The symptoms of this malady can be recognized when we begin to know all there is to know about joy, but there's no joy in our families. We know all there is to know about forgiveness, but we just can't seem to forgive our spouse!

One of the best ways to bridge this discrepancy is through small groups. In these huddles of friends, we can support one another, graciously remind one another and hold each other accountable to what we believe. All pretenses fall to a minimum when you get up close and personal!

5.

We believe that every member is a minister who has been given gifts to be discovered, developed, and deployed. We are a gift based, volunteer-driven church. Each believer will find his greatest joy and fulfillment when serving in his gifts and passion. Every believer is created for ministry, gifted for ministry, authorized for ministry, and needed for ministry (Mk. 10:45; Eph. 2:10; Ro. 12; 1 Cor. 12:14-20).

No one is unimportant! Everyone is a 10 ... somewhere! God has deposited within each of us one or more gifts through which we can make an eternal contribution! As each person finds his or her place and begins serving through their gifts, you will find maximum effectiveness and minimum weariness.

6.

We believe that God is worthy of our very best. Therefore, a growing spirit of excellence should permeate every activity. Not perfection, but excellence with consistent evaluation and a willingness to improve for the sake of the Kingdom of God are distinctive of growing ministries (Ps. 78:72; Dan. 5:12; Col. 3:17; Eccl. 10:10).

There is no greater vision, no more compelling an invitation than to serve the King of Kings! He indeed is worthy of our very best. We serve an excellent God, and since we are created in His image. Therefore, we get to be an excellent people.

That excellence will be firstly communicated not necessarily in our actions but by the heart behind our actions.

7.

We believe that genuine love and caring relationships are key to the life of every endeavor. Refusing to give audience to a spirit of complaining, we will instead be courageous in solving every problem in a way that honors God and builds biblical character. We value healthy relationships by protecting the unity of the Spirit in our church (Jms. 1:2,3; 1 Pt. 8:8-9; 1 Cor. 13:8; Ro. 16:17; Eph. 4:3).

One common element in all growing churches is problems! Yes, problems come with the territory. Growing pains, crowded parking, long lines, and short-handed classrooms will be a common companion to 21st century ministries. Yet we have chosen that complaining will not be an option. We must face and confront every problem head on, in a timely fashion and be courageous in solving each impasse. This is to be done in such way that will honor the Lord and will result in biblical character formation.

8.

We believe that the most effective evangelism happens through people inviting people. We believe that a life will reach a life. Each believer develops genuine relationships with friends and family and extends an invitation to them. Evangelism gets to be a normal, a natural lifestyle of winning others to Christ, one by one (Pr. 11:30; Jn. 1:43-45; Jn. 4:28-30).

The greatest evangelist is not a D.L. Moody, Billy Graham, or the pastor of a church. The greatest evangelists are the individuals who make up the church. Each person has unchurched loved ones, friends or family members, each needing the saving grace of Jesus Christ. Through these genuine relationships, a verbal witness is given, an invitation extended, and a non-churched person becomes willing to investigate Christianity.

I remember Sue Anne. She is a member on fire with the excitement of a new believer. We were at a Rotary Convention when I saw her seated, conversing with an elderly Japanese gentleman at a table. Although much younger than he, they seemed to be old friends. I made my way over to greet her. She immediately introduced me to Mr. Hatada.

"Mr. Hatada, this is my pastor, Wayne Cordeiro." She continued. "Mr. Hatada, do you go to church anywhere?"

"No," he replied. "I am a Buddhist."

Sue Ann, oblivious to his attempt to dodge her question, unhesitatingly continued. "Then you MUST come to our church!"

I chuckled under my breath at her somewhat disconnected reply. Mr. Hatada, presuming that she misunderstood, repeated his answer.

"No," he defended. "You see, I'm a Buddhist."

"That's OK!" she said with a tone of optimism. "You just have to come to our church! Even just once! Just come. You'll love it! You won't be the same!"

"Well, I have my own religion," he said. "It is giving money to charitable organizations like the Boy Scouts and the United Way."

"That's great!" Sue Ann shot back. "But you just HAVE to come to our church!"

"But I golf on Sundays."

"That's fine, but you must come to our church!"

By this time, I was becoming intrigued with this unique method of evangelism. For 20 minutes she gave the same reply to every one of his arguments. Whatever reason he gave as to his unwillingness or inability to accept her invitation, Sue Ann remained gracious but unwavering.

"That's fine, Mr. Hatada, but you just HAVE to come to our church!"

I remember chuckling to myself, "You can't teach this in an Evangelism course. This comes straight from the heart!"

You see, when people are excited about what God is doing in their church, evangelism becomes a natural byproduct!

9.

We believe in identifying and training emerging leaders who are fully committed to Christ and who will reach their generation with the Gospel. God is raising up men and women who will take the baton of godly character, authentic faith, and servant-hearted leadership into the next generation (2 Tim. 2:2; 1 Tim. 3:1; Titus 1:5-9; Ps. 78:6-7).

The ultimate test of a successful leader is not necessarily found in what he does but in what others are doing as a result of what he does. This core value is a constant reminder to give life away, to increase the base of leadership, and to unselfishly live to make others successful.

The Heart and Passion of New Hope

These nine core values in tandem with the Mission Statement make up the heart and passion of New Hope Christian Fellowship. This is the premise upon which all that we do is based. It establishes our "culture" in every ministry or project. It is our goal for every member to own these values so much that it permeates everything they do and say.

These values grew out of a host of discussions about what we valued. I talked with dozens of leaders, received input from as many as I could, and tested them over and again by getting feedback. By identifying these values, it helped me to clarify what was truly important and where we should be focusing our energies and resources.

Each church must find their own course, their own race, and their own calling. Then, and only then, will we be able to confidently set our compasses and navigate the ocean of decisions that will be encountered.

In scientific research, we know that when our basic premise is incorrect then all subsequent conclusions will likewise be wrong. This holds true not only in the scientific process but in churches as well. If our premise, our purpose, or our values are unsure, then every conclusion thereafter will follow suit. Our confidence in our calling will be shaky at best.

Set your compass according to God's instructions. Hammer out your purpose and assignment until that certain trumpet blows absolutely clear. Then, with confidence, you'll be able to run the race.

And when you run the right race headed in the right direction, you'll have a much better chance of finishing well! ✗

CHAPTER SEVEN STUDY GUIDE

"Setting Your Compass"

1. What is your church's statement of purpose? Can you write it from memory?

2. If you are a ministry leader in your church, write a vision statement for your ministry making sure that it is in line with the church's overarching Vision Statement.

3. If you've been to a conference lately, what are some "hammering techniques" that you have learned? Why are these better than buying ready-made trumpets?

4. What are some reasons for establishing core values early on in a ministry? What will these values help you to do?

Building Teams

Chapter Eight
Building Teams

Building teams doesn't begin with a certain kind of technique. It begins with a certain kind of heart.

⬥ ⸺ ▪ ⸺ ⬥

Doing Church as a Team is a whole new mindset for our churches today. If we are going to be a church of the 21st century, there's just no other way! The days of the Lone Ranger are over. Often in the Bible, God refers to us as the body of Christ. "Our bodies have many parts, but the many parts make up only one body when they are all put together. So it is with the body of Christ" (1 Cor. 12:12 LB). The better we understand this metaphor, the more we will be able to cooperate with God's design for the Church!

The church is not an "organization." It is more like an "organism" with living parts that must move and work together as a whole. Each individual part cannot stand on its own. If I cut off my arm and planted it in dirt, that arm would not grow into a new body. It would die! So it is with the body of Christ. Each of us has an individual assignment and role, but apart from the rest of the body, we are useless. God created it that way. That is HIS design, not ours!

If you look a bit deeper, you will notice that each part of a body works in groups. For example, the hand works with five fingers, a palm, a wrist, forearm muscles, tendons connecting them all together, etc. The composite integration of all these elements working together gives agility and coordination. You see it works best as a team, especially when all of its parts serve in harmony and cooperation toward a common goal!

Have you ever watched a concert pianist moving his fingers in perfect synchronization, running arpeggios up and down the keys of a piano? Each sinew, each ligament, every finger, muscle and joint work together in creating a symphony of notes blended together in beautiful harmony. No one finger could accomplish what the score called for. The wrist couldn't do it alone, and neither could the arm. But working together, each part fulfilling its role, the concert hall is filled with magnificent music that enthralls the hearts of everyone present.

This is the church! Connected to the "Head, Who is Christ" (Eph. 4:15), and working together for the "common good" (1 Cor. 12:7). Each of us is to be a living, functioning, serving member of the body of Christ. God has gifted each of us with talents and abilities. He has divinely endowed us and has given us all we need to serve His purposes, but always remember: we do it best in teams.

Building teams does not begin with a certain kind of technique. It begins with a certain kind of heart. This is an unselfish, authentic heart, desiring only God's best. It constantly asks the question, "How can I include others?"

It anticipates the joy of sharing experiences, struggles, and victories. It realizes that like the body, we work best in teams. That's the way God designed us to function the best.

Fractal Team Building

I owe much of the understanding of this metaphor to a long time friend, Loren Cunningham, the president and founder of Youth With a Mission. The first time I met him was in Hilo a decade and a half ago. He's a big man, over six feet tall and well over the 200 pound mark. I remember the first time I shook his hand. Mine disappeared in his and I was secretly glad to get it back. His heart is as big as he is.

Last summer, Loren was visiting Hawaii. We were having lunch together in Waikiki on a balmy Sunday afternoon with a good friend, Danny Lehman joining us. During the meal, I asked Loren if he wouldn't mind sharing some ideas he had garnered along the way on equipping God's people to reach the lost. That one question ignited three hours of brisk interchange and conversation. He shared with me a seed thought about "fractal patterns" that he had heard Winkey Pratney discuss in one of his seminars. We sat and talked until it looked like the waiter was about to charge us double for loitering.

This process of building teams is by no means the only way. There are dozens of time tested ways to build teams, and no one way is necessarily the best. Find which works best for you and do it! The bottom line is this: you can't do it alone! You weren't designed to. So what you will read over these next few pages is the way we have found that works well for us. We're still hammering it out, but it works splendidly for our style and make up.

The Church: A Living Organism

According to Webster's, the word fractal means: "Any curves or shapes for which any suitably chosen part is similar in shape to a given larger or smaller part when magnified or reduced to the same size."

Now if you're anything like me, I was just as much in the dark after discovering the definition as I was before! Let me see if I can explain it as it pertains to doing church as a team.

Living organisms are in some aspects, very similar to organization, while in other ways, they are very different. For instance, they both require structure, direction, measurable objectives, and leadership. On the other hand, an organism is a living entity with emotions, changes, natural growth, and a susceptibility to diseases, accidents, predators, and sicknesses.

The Church, or the "body of Christ," is a living organism. It may have organizational needs, but organization alone would cause it to be unhealthy. It could look fine on the outside but lifeless on the inside. It's the same with the difference between silk plants and live ones. The silk plants look wonderful from a distance, but up close, you can tell there's no life or fragrance to it.

Sometimes, it seems easier to treat the Church as an organization because, like silk plants, once they've been arranged, the maintenance is nil. They look good, but don't get too close! Recall with me the fig tree in Mark, "And seeing at a distance a fig tree in leaf, He went to see if perhaps He would find anything on it; and when He came to it, He found nothing but leaves..." (Mark 11:13). Later, Jesus actually cursed the fig tree and it withered up! The tree looked good from a distance, but up close, there was no evidence of fruit.

The fractal design is more akin to living organisms than anything I have seen so far. It's a simple concept that works. This structure is one that repeats itself over and over again.

The Repeating Pattern

Take the example of a fern. Here in Hawaii, we see these plants growing everywhere, and it lends us a wonderful example of this type of structure. If you look at the fern plant in its entirety, you will see one major stem with smaller branches extending from it on either side. Now take a closer look at one of the branches. You will see the same structure duplicated with a major stem and smaller leaves extending. If your eyesight is good, observe closely one of the individual leaves. You will see that very same structure duplicated again with a major vein running down the middle of the leaf with several more extending from it. If you had a microscope, you'd see that structure duplicated again until every cell is reached.

Our bodies have that same fractal design. Physically, you'll see one major unit called the human body with limbs extending. Take one of the limbs, and you'll see within it a major artery with several branching of it. Then take one of the secondary arteries and you will see again several more branching off until every area of the body is reached for circulation and health.

Doing church as a team uses this same fractal design. It is a very simple, duplicable pattern that is found in most organisms. Each one has similar patterns and similar purposes. For the sake of simplicity, we build teams in groupings of five (and if working with couples, the total count would be ten). The reason for this is that it seems to work best for appropriate spans of care.

Growth is Downward

Simply, here's how it works. As an example, let's say I am asked to help with the children's ministry. My passion is to work with kids and I have some teaching gifts and organizational skills. I would love to work with the children, so I say "yes."

In doing church as a team, my first move is not to jump in and start working with the children. Instead, my first step is to build a team of four leaders with whom I will serve. When I choose the four, we have a team totaling five people with similar passions and supportive gifts. The following is a graph that illustrates this:

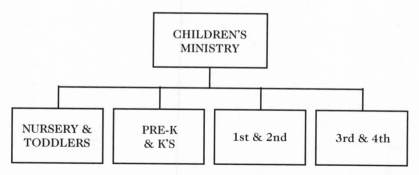

Now let's say that the ages will be birth through fourth graders. So we form our teams which are: 1) Nursery & Toddlers, 2)Pre K's and Kindergarten, 3) First and Second grade, and finally, 4) Third and Fourth grade.

Using the fractal design, I find a person who loves babies. When this nursery and toddlers leader says "yes" to be part of the children's ministry team, the first thing he or she does is NOT to jump in and start working with the babies. Duplicating the pattern of what was just done, the leader builds a team of four other leaders with similar passions and supporting gifts. So another team is built to serve in the nursery and toddlers. The exact same thing is done with the Pre-Ks and Kindergarten, the First and Second Grade team, and the Third and Fourth as well. Here's an example of how it would look when one of the four leaders (Nursery and Toddler's leader) builds a team:

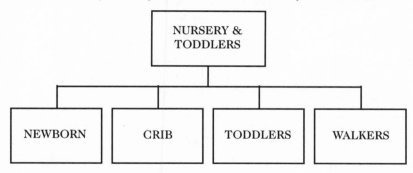

Each of the other leaders does exactly the same thing, duplicating the team building process. Then, if you add all the teams up (the four main leaders each serving with four on their individual teams), the leadership of the children's ministry grows immediately to twenty-one people. And that's just going "two deep." This pattern can continue by duplicating this to a third or even a fourth level. As large as the ministry grows, the teams can simply grow deeper.

You see, with this pattern of ministry, growth is "downward" which is to say that the larger the ministry grows, the deeper the levels of teams you build. For example, if the Nursery & Toddlers has its four leaders (1: Newborns, 2: Crib, 3: Toddlers, and 4: Walkers) and the Lord increases the ministry three-fold. What do we do? Relax! We no longer need to stress or burn the midnight oil of worry. In the fractal design, the leader of the "newborns" finds four other leaders and they do the very same thing his ancestors did! That's right. He or she chooses four leaders with similar passions and supportive gifts to form another level of leadership. Growth is downward.

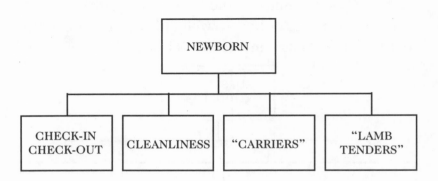

This can go on indefinitely, and you can get as creative as needed. In this way, every person is included, and every person has a role to fill.

But remember! Regardless of how large the ministry grows, God will always provide the servants necessary for the assignment. Look for them in the forest. They are there!

Growth Without Burn-Out

Here's another wonderful aspect of this design. As the leader of the children's ministry, I will primarily serve with four other leaders: the Nursery and Toddlers leader, the Pre K's & Kindergarten leader, the First and Second Grade leader, and the Third and Fourth Grade leader. These four people comprise my team. Now as the ministry grows, how many leaders will I personally oversee?

Four.

What if the ministry doubles and we have to go deeper in our leadership base by two more levels? How many will I personally oversee if the ministry grows from ten nursery children to one hundred?

Four.

What if it grows to two hundred?

Still four.

That's right. The answer will always be four! Each leader will always be overseeing four others. In this way, no one burns out! You care for four people, or a team of five (yourself included, of course!) You see, in New Hope, the growth is always downward. The larger the ministry, the deeper the leadership base goes.

Natural Discipleship Groupings

Here's another aspect of the genius of this design. Each team falls into natural groupings of five. These can become "discipleship groups," each formed because of similar passions and similar paths of ministry. Due to the natural pattern of groupings, this may be the easiest and simplest way to begin a small groups ministry! By seeing your leaders as your small group, then the common tasks become much more than a responsibility to be fulfilled. Each person can be individually cared for and nurtured by the leader. Likewise, each of the four leaders will have their own groups of four. In this way, each one is being nurtured while at the same time they themselves are nurturing four others.

With the fractal design, our church becomes not a church with small groups, but a church of small groups. Here, people are accountable to a leader, and that leader is accountable as well. Each one is discipling others as well as being discipled themselves.

Simplifying the Design

Similar to the math classes I used to take in high school, I like to boil everything down to its lowest common denominator. I understand everything more clearly in its simplest form, so that's what we did. Using the principles of fractal leadership, we simplified the form so you can teach it to your teams. Learning this one idea is foundational to everything we do. Whether you are beginning a new ministry or taking part in an existing one, understanding the process of building teams will certainly be helpful. I like to use pictures, so here's how I personally present the fractal design.

Step One

The first step in building your team, whether it's starting a new ministry or building another level in an existing one, is to always begin by drawing a circle.

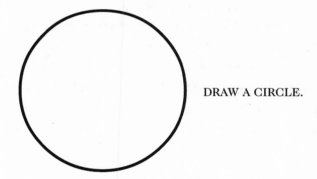

DRAW A CIRCLE.

That's it. Simply draw a circle. This circle represents the outer parameters of your ministry. In concept, this is everything you will be responsible for.

If you are overseeing the children's ministry, this circle embraces everything that is connected to that ministry. If you are a senior pastor, this represents everything about the church and its ministry: the services, pastoral care, leadership, counseling, discipleship, finances, organization, facilities, and more. In other words, everything! If you are a volunteer overseeing the ushering ministry, this would include the passing out of bulletins, seating people and seeing to their needs. If you are a volunteer who directs the hospitality ministry, this circle will represent everything that the hospitality ministry includes: known or as yet unknown to you!

That's right. At this point, you may not know all that is contained within this circle. But don't worry. You'll discover them along the way. This simply sets the parameters or the boundaries of your role.

Step Two

The second step is to draw a cross in the middle of the circle. Picture it as if you were looking through the scope of a rifle. It should resemble the "cross-hairs" in the lens. This shows you what you are aiming at. In fact, that is exactly what this step is for.

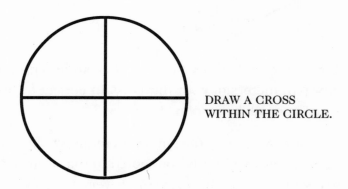

DRAW A CROSS
WITHIN THE CIRCLE.

At this point, write down the purpose for your ministry. What is its intention, the God-glorifying purpose for what you are doing? Each ministry within the church should know its purpose with clarity and precision. Keep in mind the heart of the "Great Commission" along with the church's overarching Mission Statement. Then, in one or two sentences, articulate why you are embarking on this venture. What is the goal of this ministry? What should it accomplish that will put this ministry in synch with the overall direction of the church?

Here are a few mission statements or "aims" in New Hope:

Front Lines Ministries
To present the Gospel to non-Christians and Christians alike with simplicity and excellence. With the Holy Spirit's direction, we will redeem the arts for the glory of God and present the Gospel in contemporary ways that will reach the heart.

Midweek Community Services
To develop mature, fruitful, soul-winning leaders.

New Hope "Seeds Ministry"
The purpose of the Seeds Ministry is to be a source of supply and support that builds up the Body of Christ within, and to provide tools to reach out for the furtherance of the Great Commission.

Missions
Extending the heart of New Hope beyond Hawaii's borders for evangelism and bridge building.

Graphic Arts Ministry
Equipping the church with excellent and effective visual tools for communicating the Gospel of Jesus Christ.

This step is crucial in doing church as a team. It gives everyone the same starting point in understanding how it all fits together. Without it, individuals will be building from different sets of blueprints. Then, regardless of how sincere or how hard each one is trying; there will inevitably be colliding expectations. This is why some ministries spend more of their time putting out personality fires than in doing the ministry. Why? Because they were inadvertently "aiming" at different targets. The purpose must be identified. The clearer the target, the better the chances we will have of hitting it!

Step Three

The next step begins by asking these questions:

- If this ministry (project, responsibility or ministry) were broken into four separate quadrants, what would they be?

- What would I call each one?

- Would the combination of these four encapsulate the total responsibilities needed to fulfill this ministry?

- If so, what would each be titled?

Title each quadrant with a heading that will describe its purpose. The combination of these four should match the purpose statement you have just written. Likewise, your purpose statement should be in alignment with the overall statement of purpose for the church. (At the end of this chapter, there will be some work sheets for you to take some time to practice these steps.) New Hope Christian Fellowship's circle that encompasses the whole ministry looks something like this:

Step Four

The fourth step is to determine what gifts or gift mix would make the best fit for a person overseeing each quadrant. Would a gift of evangelism be necessary for someone serving as a leader in outreach events? Absolutely.

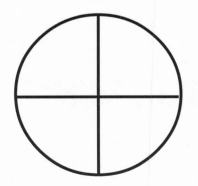

DETERMINE WHAT GIFTS ARE REQUIRED WITHIN EACH QUADRANT.

What about temperament? Would this person need to be primarily a "task-oriented" or more of a "people-oriented" person? Would this person best fit into the task if he were an introvert or an extrovert? All the aspects of a person's "DESIGN" should be taken into consideration for the best possible fit.

Let's take a look at the distinction between an introvert and an extrovert for a moment.

Introverts and Extroverts

An extrovert loves people, and when he is with people, they charge up his batteries. When he is isolated from them, his batteries drain. An introvert also loves people, however when he is with people, they have a tendency to drain his batteries. He has to isolate himself periodically to charge them back up.

Although, I'm an introvert, I'm right at the edge of being an extrovert. I do need time alone to recharge my batteries, but I am close enough to being an extrovert that when I'm with people, my batteries drain very slowly. If I am isolated for any extended length of time, I go stir crazy.

I remember when I was in the sixth grade; we were living in Japan. The winters were bitter cold. I attended a small military school in a nearby town called Sagamihara. Miss Anne Clifford was the sixth grade teacher. She was as tall as the school flagpole and as mean as they come. Believe it or not, from time to time, I would get disciplined by the teacher (for some silly, unfair and concocted reason, I'm sure). Her method of discipline took the form of confining me to the coat closet for fifteen minutes per trumped up charge.

Sitting in the dark for the first five minutes was tolerable, but at that point in my incarceration, I'd start to go crazy. I would rather she had tortured me with bamboo splinters under my fingernails. When I couldn't stand it any longer, I'd begin pacing the floor, counting the number of boards it took from one end to the other. Next I would try on all the coats, go through their pocket for any leftover candies, or switch different kid's boots with other kid's coats, making new and curious combinations.

You see, my temperament is such that I have to be with people. I hate being cooped up alone. I have to fellowship, talk and be with others.

In the same way, God knows your design, and He wants to match your ministry with your make-up, your temperament with your tasks. God knew my design, and that's the reason I am the way I am. If you don't like the way I am, don't blame me. It's God's fault! (You may laugh here.)

Step Five

In this step, identify the possible people who might fit these gift combinations. Ask yourself who would be the best. Talk to those who may know or who may have seen these different individuals in action. Do your best to fit the names with the gifts required, temperament needed, and maturity necessary for the task or position. When this step is completed well, the chances will be greater for a lasting and fruitful experience in ministry.

Step Six

The final step in slotting new and emerging leaders is to ASK! Don't wait for them to somehow magically appear uniformed and ready for duty. Challenge the ones you think would fit. Because you've already done the research, many of those asked may be excited to comply!

God has someone for each ministry He initiates, so don't force wrong pieces into slots by not doing your homework first. Guard yourself from the tendency to simply fill a position with a "warm body." Follow this process. It will spare you many pains later on!

But ask! Especially if you genuinely feel that it may release someone's dream! It is astonishing what you can accomplish by simply asking. Not only will you often receive what you ask for, but also many times I have experienced the other person thanking me for having taken the initiative!

Jesus did that. He asked. He found some potential disciples and asked each of them saying, "Come, follow Me." In Matthew 7:7, Jesus further instructs us to ask the Father for what we need. "Ask, and it shall be given to you; seek, and you shall find; knock, and it shall be opened to you."

One reason we may shy away from asking is fear. We worry about the outcome. We are concerned about offending or bothering people, or that they might perceive us as weak. Maybe even worse, they might perceive us as attempting to take advantage of our relationship with them.

Relax! On the contrary, it is actually quite arrogant and self-righteous to assume that others aren't willing to help or assist. They very well might just be waiting to be asked!

Here's a key in your asking someone to join up. You must be genuinely sincere in your belief that you want to see him or her grow and be used in wonderful ways by the Holy Spirit! You must be completely authentic in your invitation.

One final note of reminder as we close this chapter. I am sure that you are a nice person and very capable. But, quite frankly, you NEED people in ministry. You cannot develop the perfect ministry. You cannot come up with all the creative ideas yourself. There are plenty of others who are as gifted, if not more so, than you! There are plenty of others willing to pitch in and offer their expertise, advice, and assistance! When I get together with some of our staff and we gang up on tackling a problem, there's nothing we can't solve! Moreover, they spark all kinds of new ideas in me and my creative juices start to overflow! ✗

CHAPTER EIGHT STUDY GUIDE

"Building Your Team"

Practice building teams by doing each of the six steps:

1. What is the first step?

   _____

   _____

2. Next, draw the circle with cross hairs. What do the cross hairs represent?

   _____

   _____

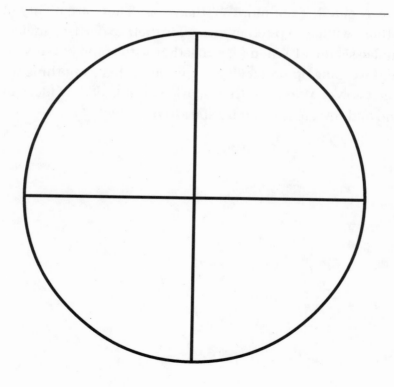

Write out the aim or purpose of the team you are building:

_____

_____

_____

3. Next, title your four quadrants:

    Quadrant One:

    _____

    Quadrant Two:

    _____

    Quadrant Three:

    _____

    Quadrant Four:

    _____

4. List the general gifts necessary for each quadrant:

    1. _____

    2. _____

    3. _____

    4. _____

5. Write the names of possible leaders for each quadrant in the spaces below:

1. _____

2. _____

3. _____

4. _____

6. Are you an introvert or an extrovert? On the continuum below, place an "X" where you think you fall.

EXTREME INTROVERT   MILD   EXTREME EXTROVERT

0

7. Covering up the graph above, ask a friend or spouse to place an "X" on the graph below where they believe you fall.

EXTREME INTROVERT   MILD   EXTREME EXTROVERT

0

CHAPTER NINE

Nurturing the Team

Nurturing the Team

◆——┤——◆

An Atmosphere of Health

I have three children. Over the years I have watched them grow in height as well as in maturity. There's one obvious thing I have noticed about growth. You don't have to force it or plead with it to happen. It does so on its own! If there is a healthy atmosphere and the food is nutritious, barring the intrusion of any life-threatening disease or accident, growth is usually a natural thing! In fact, if everything is fairly healthy and growth is not occurring, then I get worried!

Churches are designed to be greenhouses for budding leaders with potential dreams in their hearts. An atmosphere of health is one of the simplest, yet most overlooked factor in growing healthy people and healthy leaders. New Hope is no exception to that rule.

Living to Make Others Successful

One of the principles in doing church as a team is found in the fact that, as leaders, we live to make the others in our team successful, not vice versa! If each member is healthy and fulfilled, then the ministry benefits. If they are successful, people will be helped. It is absolutely necessary to cultivate a selfless spirit and live to make the other person successful.

Quite frankly, that's exactly how our body works. My lungs cheer for my heart to be healthy and to work well. Why? Not only for the heart's sake, but also for the lung's sake! You see, if the heart goes down, my lungs do, too. My stomach wants my kidneys to function well, and it also wants the liver to be in top form. Not only for their sakes, but also for its own sake.

As a pastor, I need everyone in the church to be functioning well. This is not only for their sakes, but also for my health! You see, if the set up crew doesn't function well, come Sunday morning, I am in trouble! If the Front Lines Team drops out or has internal struggles, it affects everything else in the Sunday services. What if the children's ministry falters? It throws everything else off kilter! It is absolutely critical that all the members be healthy so everyone else will be healthy as well!

We live to make each other successful. That's the deal.

Steward Your Authority Well

"For this reason I am writing these things while absent, in order that when present I may not use severity, in accordance with the authority which the Lord gave me, **for building up and not for tearing down**" (2 Cor. 13:10 emphasis mine).

This one truth will transform your people skills. Paul explains the purpose for authority. It is for building people up, not for tearing them down! He echoes that in 2 Cor. 10:8 with these words, "...authority, which the Lord gave for building up and not for destroying you..." God has no problem giving us authority if we will use it for what He's designed it for, to build people up! It is a gift to encourage the best in people, not a tool for leveraging people in order to fulfill our desires.

I remember when I was in Bible College. I was just starting off in the ministry, and I was asked to sing at one of our denomination's conventions. Being a novice as well as a young Christian, it took all I had to just stand in front of this dignified group of pastors and leaders. I was so nervous until this day, I can't even remember the song I sang. What I do remember was after the session was through, one of the most respected pastors in the denomination motioned to me and sat me down. Because of his authority and my deep respect for him, his words were indelibly etched into my soul.

"Wayne, I know you were nervous tonight, but I want you to know how impressed I was by your sincerity. You conquered your nervousness because you wanted to exalt the Lord more than anything else in the world! And it showed. God has His hand on you, and because you want to please Him, He will use you in wonderful ways. He has great things in store for you. Keep singing. Keep speaking to people of His great love."

Those simple but sincere words impacted me tremendously. Over the next three years, I recorded my first album of original songs, traveled each summer for the Bible College (which paid for my tuition and room & board) and went into Youth for Christ as a youth evangelist for seven years after graduation! Much of that began because of one pastor who stewarded his authority and took the time to encourage a wet-behind-the-ears Bible School student.

Now one of my friends could have encouraged me by saying "great job" with a pat on the back. That would have been nice. But when someone in authority uses the same to build you up, you can go on that for years!

Do you want more authority? Here's a simple way to build it. Start building people up! It's just that simple. When God sees that you are willing to use whatever authority you have to encourage the best out of others. He will give you more! My prayer is that our churches will be filled with great authority as we see God's people's dreams coming true in their desires to be all they can be for the King!

The Three "C's" of Healthy Churches

Let me give you the three "C's" of a healthy church atmosphere. I learned this at one of Bill Hybels' seminars on leadership. Bill and his wonderful staff of Willow Creek Association are unselfish servants in their desire to see the local church increase in fruitfulness.

Cause

The first "C" stands for the *cause* behind why the church exists! Cause is to a church as an engine is to an automobile. It is that which fuels their passion and activities. It gives the motivation to overcome the hills and valleys every ministry encounters along the way. It is the bottom line by which all else can be measured.

May I be so bold to suggest that this cause is *evangelism*! Without lost people coming to a saving knowledge of Jesus Christ, all our efforts would be in vain. We might have wonderful Bible studies, great potlucks, outstanding small groups, and magnificent Sunday services. But unless people are giving their hearts to Jesus, what would all our activities amount to? Granted, discipleship and Bible Studies are absolutely critical to building people, but never to the exclusion of winning the lost! I often remind those in New Hope of the reason for our weekend services. Because of our heart for the lost, we don't have Sunday services to maintain the convinced. Instead the weekend services is to "partner with each member in their attempts to reach their friends and family for Christ."

The cause for why we exist must never be compromised or deprioritized. On a scale of one to ten, this should be bouncing up above the eight-mark. Nothing adds excitement and an atmosphere of celebration to a church like a consistent in-flow of new believers! If people are not coming to know Christ, we immediately rethink what we are doing and retool!

Let me take you back for a moment to our statement of purpose. If you recall, it states that New Hope exists: "To present the Gospel in such a way that turns non-Christian into converts..." Therefore, if people are not coming to know Christ as their Lord and Savior, then we are not "presenting the Gospel *in such a way*..." The Gospel never changes, but the cultures do. Therefore, our style must accurately address the culture to which we've been called. This includes our music, facilities, parking, greeters, ambiance, activities, everything! Yes, everything matters when it comes to reaching people with the Gospel of Christ. Whether or not they can understand the Gospel in such a way that it results in them giving their hearts to Jesus is of utmost importance to us. Whatever must be recalibrated so that this happens, we will do it!

The cause of evangelism must always remain strong.

Community

A second factor found in healthy churches is something called *community*. This word depicts the free interchange, the open fellowship, and genuine relationships that glue people together. It has little to do with programs or activities, and much more with what happens between people *during* these programs or activities.

In John's first epistle, we find him alluding to this principle of community; " ... if we walk in the light as He Himself is in the light, we have fellowship with one another, and the blood of Jesus His Son cleanses us from all sin" (1 Jn. 1:7). This fellowship is what binds people together. It is this sense of community that brings depth to a congregation, adds life to activities, and turns a crowd into a family. This is where life is found. No matter how many gatherings, ministries, projects, or concerts a church has, without *life* within each one, the activity is useless.

In the absence of community, a church might easily become a high octane, crusade-driven ministry, or it can fall victimized by entropy and end up becoming a "keeper of the traditions." Community is the life, the gel that fuses hearts together.

I remember, some years ago in Hilo, when we were in the middle of our building program. We purchased a twenty-acre lot, and after a few years, had raised enough money to begin building. I recall the day we poured the cement for our fellowship hall. It was an area larger than that of a gymnasium, so this was to be no small task! Fifty men gathered at early dawn on a Saturday. We each had on a pair of rubber boots and the oldest, most disposable clothes we could find. The trucks began arriving at 7 a.m. The sun rose like a golden disk, watery at first, but then it began burning our skin with an increasing strength as the morning wore on. Before long, beads of sweat were rolling off our foreheads only to be mixed into the concrete. We ate a late lunch provided by the ladies from the church as the cement cured in mid afternoon. At the close of our project, we kicked off our boots and sat in huddles summarizing the events of the day. We laughed, chided each other, and relived every single minute of the pour, over and over and over again. By the time we had washed our trowels and headed for home, it was dark.

Looking back over that day, the most endearing memories I have are not of the pour itself, but what happened between our hearts during the pour. We arrived as brothers in Christ, and by the end of the day; we left not only as brothers, but also as friends. The pour was not an end in itself, but a means of achieving something much more eternal!

It's called ... life!

Community happens when there's a sense of celebration and relationship regardless of the activity. It happens when each gathering takes on the atmosphere of a family reunion where hugs are abundant and bursts of laughter come easily. It happens when people begin to enjoy just being with one another, where the atmosphere is more than just "friendly."

In a recent study, it was found that when people go to a church, they are not just looking for friendly people. They are looking for friends. That one quality requires a genuine willingness to open your life and let another in. It is absolutely crucial to guard this quality.

On a scale of one to ten, this too must be bouncing above eight.

Corporate

The third quality of a healthy church is healthy *corporate* finances! Not necessarily abundant finance but the wise stewardship of what is there. Paying the rent, turning on lights, and staying current with the monthly bills all require adequate finances and good stewardship.

The area of stewardship is more important than most realize. Look at what Jesus says in Luke 16:11: "If therefore you have not been faithful in the use of unrighteous mammon, who will entrust the true riches to you?" According to the way Jesus sees it, the way we handle finances as a church will determine whether we will be faithful with "true riches." Should those true riches be influence, spiritual gifts, or authority, our stewardship over what He has given us acts like a boot camp for things eternal.

All three of these graphs need to be vigilantly monitored. When one or more of these graphs begin to slump, energy and action need to be immediately expended to remedy the situation. Our goal is to keep all three graphs bouncing above the eighty percentiles.

A Final Word

There is so much yet to be learned. I am still writing this book. As time goes on, I will add to it. Often, I feel as if I am in the kindergarten stage of learning how to shepherd God's people and build leaders who will catch the heart and vision of Jesus Christ for the lost. This world is crying out for godly leaders who have taken the time to develop a spirit of excellence with an ongoing desire to receive advice and remain teachable.

I love what God is beginning to do in the churches. There is a new wine being poured out, and only hearts made of new wineskins will be able to survive the pour! The others will burst and lose their contents, being left with ornate, but empty wineskins.

Some time ago, I went to watch a movie. The story line was magnificent and over the hour or so that I watched it, a tapestry of people and events was spun before my eyes. It was a wonderful experience.

On the way out, being a curious sort of person who loves to see how things work, I walked up a short flight of stairs and poked my nose into the projection room. The film that captured the wonderful story I just experienced was contained in two large, round canisters. It must have been a mile or two of film with each frame holding a tiny portion of the story in its celluloid embrace.

The light rays of the projector had cast its beam onto the screen while frame after frame rolled steadily before it. Frame after frame after frame. The quick but steady pace of the frames passing gives the images a "moving" quality; hence the inaugural name of the "moving picture" shows (as they were called during my grandfather's days).

Now, suppose you stopped one of the frames and held it still before the projector lens. You would see an image in suspended animation. Seeing that one frame alone without the rest of the frames marching in cadence before the light's beam wouldn't give you much understanding of the movie.

You would need that one frame moving in sequence with the many other frames in order to understand the whole story.

Listen carefully. Every one of us is like a single frame in God's story. Each frame is incredibly important to God's plan. How often we think that no one would miss us if we didn't show up. If a bunch of frames decided to go on strike and walk out of the film, the movie would be hard pressed to make any sense. And we can do that as Christians. Justifying our "tiny, insignificant" existence, we simply choose not to get involved. When that happens, no wonder the picture of the church is jumpy and jerky!

But if we are serious about presenting a clear picture of the Lord to a desperate world, then we must each take our place. Be faithful in the "frame" that God has allotted to your care. Develop it with color! Then plug into the cadence of those with whom He has called you.

And as we do church as a team, you watch. You wait. You'll see one of the most beautiful and moving pictures of the heart of Jesus unfold right before your eyes!

Ho'omakaukau? Imua!

(Ready? Paddle forward!) ✘

CHAPTER NINE STUDY GUIDE

Nurturing the Team

1. What are the three "C's" of church health? What does each stand for?

C_____

C_____

C_____

2. If you are a pastor, use a scale of one to ten to rate each "C" in your church based on where you feel it currently ranks. Then, list several remedies as to how each one can be increased in effectiveness.

C_____   Rank _____

1_____

2_____

3_____

C_____   Rank _____

1_____

2_____

3_____

C_____   Rank _____

    1_____

    2_____

    3_____

3. After reading this book, I will commit to the following changes:

In my thinking:

_____

_____

_____

_____

In my ministry:

_____

_____

_____

_____

4. I am a "10!" ... somewhere.

Where am I currently serving?

_____

_____

If not, where do I plan to be involved?

_____

_____

5. Take a few minutes and write your pastor a note to let him know of your support. If you are a pastor, take time right now to send a note of appreciation to your key leaders thanking them for partnering with you in "doing church as a team."

About the Author

Wayne Cordeiro is presently the Senior Pastor of New Hope Christian Fellowship in O'ahu, a new work that was planted in September 1995. In its first three years, New Hope grew to over 5,000 at their weekend services with 3,820 receiving Christ for the first time. He has also planted twelve other churches in Hawaii, Guam, and Japan. New Hope O'ahu is currently listed as one of the fastest growing churches in the nation.

Prior to moving to O'ahu, Pastor Wayne was the Senior Pastor at New Hope Christian Fellowship in Hilo, Hawaii for almost 12 years. Under his pastoral leadership, the New Hope Hilo congregation grew from 50 to over 1,700, and moved into their 20-acre church facilities, "The Gathering Place," in October, 1992.

Wayne was raised in Palolo Valley on O'ahu and lived in Japan for three years. He then moved to Oregon where he finished his schooling and ministry training over the next 12 years. In 1975, he graduated Cum Laude from Eugene Bible College and continued graduate studies at Northwest Christian College and the University of Oregon. He served in Youth for Christ for seven years and as a staff pastor at Faith Center Foursquare Church in Eugene, Oregon for another three years before returning to Hawaii.

Pastor Wayne is a published songwriter, has released four albums and is a contributing author for church leadership books. He is heard on several radio stations in Hawaii and travels extensively throughout Hawaii, the Mainland U.S., and Japan to speak at conferences, churches, civic gatherings, prisons, high school assemblies, business forums and leadership conventions. Pastor Wayne also speaks often for businesses, companies and corporations on restructuring and growth strategies.

He has authored two other books: *Gems Along The Way* and *Rebuilding Life God's Way*. There are three other books that he is completing: *Kingdom Imagineers*, *Leadership Principles for the 21st Century*, and *Developing An Attitude That Attracts Success*.

Pastor Wayne and his wife, Anna, have three children, Amy, Aaron, and Abigail.

For further resources by Wayne Cordeiro, please contact:

New Hope Christian Fellowship O'ahu
2826 Kaihikapu St. 2nd Floor
Honolulu, Hawaii 96819
808/833-7717 fax 808/833-7706
www.newhope/hawaii.org